WILEY CPA Examination Review

2nd Edition

Focus Notes

Auditing

Mark Edward

JOHN WILEY & SONS, INC.
New York • Chichester • Weinheim • Brisbane • Singapore • Toronto

This text is printed on acid-free paper. ♾

ISBN 0-471-38959-5

Printed in the United States of America
10 9 8 7 6 5 4 3 2 1

Contents

Preface

This publication is a comprehensive, yet simplified study program. It provides a review of all the basic skills and concepts tested on the CPA exam and teaches important strategies to take the exam faster and more accurately. This tool allows you to take control of the CPA exam.

This simplified and focused approach to studying for the CPA exam can be used:

- As a handy and convenient reference manual
- To solve exam questions
- To reinforce material being studied

Included is all of the information necessary to obtain a passing score on the CPA exam in a concise and easy-to-use format. Due to the wide variety of information covered on the exam, a number of techniques are included:

- Acronyms and mnemonics to help candidates learn and remember a variety of rules and checklists
- Formulas and equations that simplify complex calculations required on the exam

- Simplified outlines of key concepts without the details that encumber or distract from learning the essential elements
- Techniques that can be applied to problem solving or essay writing, such as preparing a multiple-step income statement, determining who will prevail in a legal conflict, or developing an audit program
- Pro forma statements, reports, and schedules that make it easy to prepare these items by simply filling in the blanks
- Proven techniques to help you become a smarter, sharper, and more accurate test taker

This publication may also be useful to university students enrolled in Intermediate, Advanced and Cost Accounting, Auditing, Business Law, and Federal Income Tax classes.

Good Luck on the Exam,
Mark Edward

About the Author

Mark Edward has been preparing individuals for the CPA exam since 1971. For many years, he taught CPA review classes for various universities, including the California State University at Northridge and the University of California at Los Angeles. He currently operates the largest CPA review program in the state of California, under the name *Mark's CPA Review Course,* with corporate offices located in Culver City California.

Mark Edward serves on the board of directors for the California Society of CPAs, and is a member or officer of the Institute of Management Accountants, the American Society of Women Accountants, the National Association of Black Accountants, the American Association of Hispanic CPAs and the Association of Governmental Accountants.

Planning the Audit

Generally Accepted Auditing Standards (GAAS)

GAAS represent measures of the quality of performance of the auditor & address

- Auditor's professional qualities
- Judgment exercised by the auditor in performing audit & preparing report

Consist of 10 standards divided into 3 categories

1) General standards
    - Qualifications of auditor
    - Quality of work
2) Standards of field work
3) Standards of reporting

General Standards (3)

1) **Training and Proficiency** – The audit is to be preformed by a person or persons having adequate technical training and proficiency as an auditor.
2) **Independence** - In all matters relating to the assignment, an independence in mental attitude is to be maintained by the auditor or auditors.
3) **Professional Care** – Due professional care is to be exercised in the performance of the audit and the preparation of the report

Standards of Field Work (3)

1) **Planning and Supervision** – The work is to be adequately planned and assistants, if any, are to be properly supervised.
2) **Internal Controls** – A sufficient understanding of internal control is to be obtained to plan the audit and to determine the nature, timing, and extent of tests to be performed.
3) **Competent Evidence** – Sufficient competent evidential matter is to be obtained through inspection, observation, inquiries, and confirmations to afford a reasonable basis for an opinion regarding the financial statements under audit.

Standards of Reporting (4)

1) **Accounting Principles in Accordance with GAAP** – The report shall state whether the financial statements are presented in accordance with generally accepted accounting principles.

2) **No New Principles – Consistency** – The report shall identify those circumstances in which such principles have not been consistently observed in the current period in relation to the preceding period.

3) **Omitted Disclosures – None** – Informative disclosures in the financial statements are to be regarded as reasonably adequate unless otherwise stated in the report.

4) **Express an Opinion** – The report shall either contain an expression of opinion regarding the financial statements, taken as a whole, or an assertion to the effect that an opinion cannot be expressed. When an overall opinion cannot be expressed, the reasons therefore should be stated. In all cases where an auditor's name is associated with financial statements, the report should contain a clear-cut indication of the character of the auditor's work, if any, and the degree of responsibility the auditor is taking.

Summary of the 10 Generally Accepted Auditing Standards (GAAS)

T – Training and Proficiency

I – Independence

P – Professional Care

P – Planning and Supervision

I – Internal Control

C – Competent Evidence

A – Accounting Principles in Accordance with GAAP

N – No New Principles – Consistency

O – Omitted Disclosures – None

E – Express an Opinion

*The 10 Generally Accepted Auditing Standards spell out **Tippicanoe**, one of our favorite presidential candidates.*

Accepting the Engagement

Compliance With General Standards

1) Training & proficiency results from education & auditing experience
2) Independence required in both fact & appearance

   Independence in fact includes:
   - Intellectual honesty
   - No direct financial interest in client
   - No material indirect financial interest
3) Due professional care
   - Observation of standards of field work & reporting
   - Critical review at every level of supervision
   - Exercise professional skepticism
   - Obtain reasonable assurance

Understanding of Client's Operations, Business, & Industry

Auditor must have understanding or be able to obtain it prior to commencing the engagement

Avoid association with client whose management lacks integrity

Procedures prior to acceptance:

- Review client's financial statements
- Make inquiries of third parties such as client's attorneys & creditors
- Communication with predecessor auditor

Communication with Predecessor Auditor

Successor must make inquiries of predecessor auditor before accepting engagement

- Successor initiates communication
- Requires permission of client
- Consider implications of client's refusal

Nature of inquiries:

- Disagreements with management about audit procedures or accounting principles
- Communication with audit committee about fraud, illegal acts, or internal control
- Reason for change in auditor
- Integrity of management

Audit Committee

The client's audit committee is part of board of directors

- Directors that are not officers or employees
- Liaison between auditor & board of directors

Audit committee:

- Oversees financial reporting and disclosure process
- Hires auditor
- Reviews audit plan
- Reviews results & financial statements
- Oversees adequacy of internal control

Auditor & audit committee agree on:

- Timing, fees, & responsibilities of parties
- Overall audit plan

Communication During & After Audit

Communication about the audit:

- The auditor's responsibilities under GAAS
- Selection of & changes to accounting policies (may be communicated by management)
- Management's process for estimating (may be communicated by management)
- Adjustments proposed by auditor
- Auditor's judgment about the quality of entity's accounting principles
- Auditor's responsibility for information in documents containing audited financial statements
- Disagreements with management
- Management's consulting other accountants about accounting matters
- Items discussed with management prior to being retained
- Difficulties encountered in performing the audit

Other communication:

- Errors discovered by auditor & corrected by client
- Consequential fraud & illegal acts
- Fraud & illegal acts involving senior management
- Significant deficiencies in internal control not previously communicated

Engagement Letter

Includes clear understanding of nature of services and responsibility assumed

Understanding may be written, in the form of an engagement letter, or **ora**l and includes:

- **O**bjectives of engagement
- **R**esponsibilities of management
- **A**uditor's responsibilities
- **L**imitations of engagement

Understanding will also indicate:

- **F**inancial records and information will be made available
- **I**ndication of compliance with applicable laws and regulations
- **L**etter of representations at conclusion of field work
- **E**stablishment and maintenance of internal control
- **S**tatements are the responsibility of management

Engagement Letter (continued)

An engagement letter may also address:

- **F**ees to be charged by the auditor
- **I**mmaterial errors or fraud not expected to be found by audit
- **R**easonable assurance provided that statements are not materially misstated
- **M**aterial misstatements may not be detected

*The client opens its **files** to the CPA **firm**.*

Management's Responsibilities

The financial statements are the responsibility of management

By presenting financial statements, management is making various assertions:

- **R**ights & obligations (**R** & O) – the assets are the rights of the entity & the liabilities are the obligations of the entity at a particular date
- **A**llocation or valuation (**A** or V) – asset, liability, equity, revenue, & expense components have been included in the financial statements at appropriate amounts
- **C**ompleteness (**C**) – all accounts & transactions that should be, are included in the financial statements
- **E**xistence or occurrence (**E** or O) – assets & liabilities of the entity exist as of a particular date & recorded transactions occurred during a given period
- **D**isclosure & presentation (**D** & P) – components of the financial statements are properly classified, described, & disclosed

*He **raced** over & over to prove the assertion that he was the fastest runner*

Planning Considerations & Procedures

Audit planning – developing strategy for scope & conduct of audit based on

- Size & complexity of entity
- Auditor's experience with entity
- Auditor's knowledge of entity's business

Planning considerations:

- Entity's accounting policies
- Materiality levels
- Audit risk & planned assessed level of control risk
- Entity's business environment
- Methods of processing accounting information
- Items on financial statements prone to adjustment
- Conditions affecting audit tests
- Reports to be issued

Planning procedures:

- Determine involvement of consultants, specialists, & internal auditors
- Read current year's interim financial statements
- Coordinate assistance of entity personnel
- Discuss with firm personnel responsible for non-audit services matters affecting the audit
- Review correspondence files, prior year's working papers, permanent files, financial statements, & auditor's report
- Inquire about current business developments affecting entity
- Discuss type, scope, & timing of audit with management, board of directors, or audit committee
- Consider effects of recent pronouncements
- Establish timing of audit work
- Establish & coordinate staffing
- Compare financial statements to anticipated results
- Perform analytical procedures to identify risk areas
- Assess materiality and audit risk

Materiality

Recognizes relative importance of items to fair presentation of financial statements

- Items may be material due to high dollar amount (Quantitative)
- Items may be material due to nonmonetary significance (Qualitative)

Materiality can be measured in relation to:

- Financial statements taken as a whole
- A transaction

Materiality is matter of professional judgment

- Must plan audit to obtain reasonable assurance that financial statements are not misstated
- Misstatements could be material individually or collectively
- Materiality measurement based on smallest aggregate level

Audit Risk (AR)

AR is risk that material errors or fraud exists resulting in an inappropriate audit report

- Auditor uses judgment in establishing acceptable level of AR
- Lower acceptable level of AR achieved through obtaining more evidential matter

AR consists of inherent risk (IR), control risk (CR), & detection risk (DR)

Audit Risk (continued)

IR acknowledges that certain items are more susceptible to risk

- May be due to complexity of transactions or calculations, ease of theft, or lack of available objective information
- IR is beyond control of auditor & generally beyond control of entity

CR acknowledges that misstatements may not be prevented or detected by entity's internal control

- Entity's internal control may be poorly designed or poorly executed
- CR is beyond control of auditor but within control of entity

DR acknowledges that auditor may not detect material misstatement

- Auditor may not properly plan audit procedures
- DR is within control of auditor

Components of Audit Risk

	Increases risk	***Decreases risk***
Inherent risk	Declining industry Lack of working capital High rate of obsolescence	More profitable than industry average Low management turnover
Control risk	Ineffective internal controls Weak management oversight	Effective internal controls Strong management oversight
Detection risk	Decrease substantive testing Perform tests early in year	Increase substantive testing Select more effective tests Perform tests near year-end

Audit Risk Model

AR = IR X CR X DR

To apply model:

1) Establish acceptable level of audit risk
2) Measure inherent risk based on internal & external factors
3) Establish planned assessed level of control risk based on discussing internal control with management
    - May set control risk at maximum level
    - If control risk set below maximum, must perform tests of controls to verify assessment
4) Compute necessary level of detection risk

    DR = AR ÷ (IR X CR)

5) Determine if planned nature, timing, & extent substantive tests are adequate to provide appropriate level of detection risk

Consideration of Fraud in a Financial Statement Audit

Prevention & detection of fraud is management's responsibility

- Auditor provides reasonable assurance that financial statements are not materially misstated
- Absolute assurance prevented by fact that perpetrator generally conceals actions to make detection difficult

Types of Fraud

2 types of fraud can result in material misstatement of financial statements

1) Fraudulent financial reporting – intentional misstatements or omissions
2) Misappropriations of assets (defalcations) – embezzlement, stealing, or misuse of funds

Fraud most often committed when there is

- Pressure or incentive
- Opportunity

Fraud Risk Factors

Existence of certain factors lead auditor to conclude high risk of **fraudulent financial reporting**

Management characteristics:

- Compensation tied to aggressive results
- Excessive interest in stock prices & earnings
- Commitments made to analysts regarding achieving unrealistic forecasts
- Pursuit of minimizing earnings for tax purposes

Management's attitude toward internal control:

- Management dominated by single person or small group
- Controls not adequately monitored
- Known weaknesses not corrected timely
- Unrealistic goals set for operating personnel
- Use of ineffective accounting, technology, or internal audit staff

Fraud Risk Factors (continued)

Other management related factors:

- High turnover
- Strained relationship with auditor

Industry conditions:

- New accounting rules or requirements impairing profitability
- High degree of competition
- Declining industry
- Volatile industry

Fraud Risk Factors (continued)

Operating characteristics & financial instability of entity:

- Negative cash flows
- Need for capital
- Use of estimates that are unusually subjective or subject to change
- Related party transactions outside the ordinary course of business
- Significant or unusual transactions near year end
- Overly complex structure
- Unusual growth or profitability
- Vulnerable to changes in interest rates
- Difficult debt covenants
- Overly aggressive incentive programs
- Threat of bankruptcy, foreclosure, or takeover
- Pending transaction that will be adversely affected by poor results

Fraud Risk Factors (continued)

Existence of other factors lead auditor to conclude high risk of **misappropriation of assets**

Characteristics indicating lack of adequate control over susceptible assets:

- Operations not subject to proper oversight
- Inadequate screening of applicants for positions with access to assets
- Inadequate record keeping
- Insufficient segregation of duties with lack of independent checks
- Inappropriate system for authorizing & approving transactions
- Inadequate physical safeguards over assets
- Untimely or inappropriate documentation of transactions
- No requirement for vacations among employees performing key functions

Fraud Risk Factors (continued)

Other factors increase general risk of material misstatement of financial statements due to fraud

- Low employee morale
- Employees financially stressed
- Adverse relationship between employees & management or entity

Assessing Risk of Fraud

Risk of material misstatement due to fraud part of audit risk

- Auditor must consider existence of risk factors when designing audit procedures
- Risk factors not necessarily indicative of existence of fraud
- Factors are considered individually & collectively

Auditor should make inquiries of management regarding:

- Management's understanding of risk of fraud in entity
- Management's knowledge of fraud

Auditor may become aware of risk factors when:

- Deciding on acceptance of the engagement
- Planning the engagement
- Obtaining an understanding of internal control
- Performing fieldwork

Effects of Assessment

Upon assessment of risk of fraud, auditor may:

- Determine planned audit procedures are sufficient
- Decide to modify planned procedures

Modifications may include:

- Applying greater degree of skepticism
- Assigning higher level personnel to engagement
- Evaluating management's accounting decisions more carefully
- Increasing assessment of control risk to maximum

When modification not practical, auditor may withdraw from engagement

Performance of Audit Procedures

Misstatement in financial statements may be detected during performance of audit procedures

Auditor should evaluate whether misstatement indicates possibility of fraud

- May be immaterial & insignificant
- May be immaterial but significant due to level of parties involved
- May be material
- May not be able to determine materiality

When misstatement that indicates possibility of fraud is either material or materiality cannot be determined:

- Discuss with appropriate level of management
- Attempt to obtain additional evidence
- Suggest, perhaps, that client see attorney
- Consider withdrawing from engagement

Documentation

Assessment of risk of material misstatement due to fraud in planning engagement should be documented, including:

- Risk factors identified
- Auditor's response to risk factors
- Further response indicated by detection of risk factors during audit

Actions Resulting From Evidence of Fraud

Upon detecting evidence of fraud, auditor should:

- Notify appropriate level of management
- Inform audit committee whenever senior management involved or whenever material fraud is committed by anyone within the organization
- Disclose to third parties only to comply with legal or regulatory requirements, in response to inquiries of a successor auditor, in response to a subpoena, or in accordance with requirements for audits of entities receiving governmental financial assistance

Responsibility to Detect & Report Illegal Acts

Illegal acts may have a direct effect on financial statements or only an indirect effect

Auditor provides reasonable assurance regarding illegal acts having a direct effect on financial statements

Auditor provides no assurance regarding illegal acts having an indirect effect on financial statements

- More difficult to detect by auditor
- No assurance that such illegal acts will be detected
- No assurance that resulting contingent liabilities will be disclosed

If auditor becomes aware of possibility of illegal acts with indirect effect, procedures should be applied to determine if illegal act occurred

Responsibility to Detect & Report Illegal Acts (continued)

When auditor aware of a possible illegal act by client, auditor should:

- Obtain an understanding of the nature & circumstances
- Evaluate effect on financial statements

Circumstances may require modification of opinion

- Qualified or adverse opinion, depending on materiality, if illegal act with material effect on financial statements not properly reported or disclosed
- Disclaimer if client prevents auditor from obtaining sufficient evidence to evaluate occurrence

Refusal by client to accept a modified opinion may result in withdrawal from the engagement

Assurance Provided by Auditor

	Not material	***Material***
Errors	No assurance	Reasonable assurance
Fraud	No assurance	Reasonable assurance
Illegal acts with direct effect on financial statements	No assurance	Reasonable assurance
Illegal acts with indirect effect on financial statements	No assurance	No assurance

Consideration of Internal Control

Consideration of internal control is necessary to determine nature, timing, & extent of substantive tests

Objectives of Internal Control

A well-designed system of internal control achieves the following objectives:

- **A**ccurate reliable financial statements
- **S**afeguarding of assets
- **A**dherence with applicable laws and regulations
- **P**romotion of effective and efficient operations

*A company with weak internal control should fix it **ASAP**.*

Components of Internal Control

Internal control consists of interrelated components:

- **C**ontrol Activities
- **R**isk Assessment
- **I**nformation and Communication
- **M**onitoring
- Control **E**nvironment

*It's a **crime** when a company does not have effective internal control.*

Control Activities

Control activities are policies & procedures that help ensure that management directives are followed

The auditor will be concerned about:

- **P**erformance reviews – comparisons of actual performance to expectations
- **I**nformation processing – checks on accuracy, completeness, & authorization of transactions
- **P**hysical controls – safeguarding assets & controlling access to records
- **S**egregation of duties –reducing opportunities for one individual to commit errors & conceal them

I say! These control activities are ***pips***

Duties requiring segregation are:

- Authorization
- Recording
- Custody
- Comparison

Risk Assessment

Risk assessment addresses how the company identifies, analyzes, & manages risk

Risks relevant to preparation of financial statements are affected by internal & external events & circumstances:

- Changes in operating environment
- New personnel
- New information systems
- Rapid growth
- New technology
- New lines, products, or activities
- Corporate restructuring
- Foreign operations
- Accounting pronouncements

Entity vs Auditor Risk Assessment

Entity – designed to identify, analyze, and manage risks that affect entity's objectives

Auditor – involves assessment of inherent risk and control risk to evaluate likelihood of material misstatements occurring in financial statements

Information & Communication

Information & communication relates to the identification, capture, & exchange of information that enables individuals to carry out their responsibilities

Monitoring

Monitoring by management allows for evaluation as to whether internal control is operating as planned

Control Environment

The control environment sets the tone of the organization

Factors include:

- Commitment to **c**ompetence
- **H**uman resource policies & practices
- **O**rganizational structure
- **P**articipation of board of directors or audit committee
- **P**hilosophy & operating style of management
- **E**thical values & integrity
- Assignment of **r**esponsibility & authority

In our environment, the boss rides a ***Chopper*** *to work*

Relationship of Objectives to Risk Assessment & Control Activities

There is a relationship among objectives of internal control, risk assessment, & control activities

1) Company establishes objective

   We wish to reduce the volume of uncollectible receivables

2) Company assesses risk by evaluating factors that prevent objective from being met

   When we sell to customers with poor or incomplete credit histories, a high percentage prove uncollectible

3) Establish control activity that will help company meet objective

   If we perform a more thorough credit check on customers before selling on credit, we will reduce the number of sales made to customers with poor or incomplete credit histories, reducing uncollectible accounts

Relationship of Internal Control to Audit Procedures

The understanding of internal control has a direct impact on the nature, timing, & extent of substantive tests to be performed

Either of 2 strategies

Substantive strategy

1) Auditor sets control risk at maximum based on understanding of design of internal control
2) Auditor will not rely on internal control & does not perform tests of controls
3) Resulting detection risk is low requiring more effective substantive testing

Reliance strategy

1) Auditor sets control risk below maximum based on understanding of design of internal control
2) Auditor will rely on internal control
3) Auditor performs tests of controls to determine if assessed level of control risk is valid
4) Auditor reassesses control risk based on results of tests of control
5) Resulting detection risk may be higher requiring less substantive testing

	Substantive strategy	***Reliance strategy***
When appropriate	Internal control expected to be relatively ineffective Not cost effective to rely on internal control to reduce substantive testing	Internal control expected to be relatively effective Cost effective to rely on internal control to reduce substantive testing
Control risk	Set at maximum	Set below maximum
Tests of controls	Not required	Required
Detection risk	Relatively low	Relatively high
Substantive testing	Must be more effective	Can be less effective

Understanding the Design of Internal Control

An understanding of the design allows an auditor to assess how internal control is intended to function

The auditor must understand each of the 5 components to:

- Identify types of potential misstatements
- Consider factors that affect the risk of material misstatement
- Design substantive tests

To accomplish this, the auditor must perform procedures that will provide knowledge of:

- The design of controls for each of the 5 components as they relate to the financial statements
- Whether controls have been placed in operation and are being used by client

Understanding the Design of Internal Control (continued)

In addition to previous experience, the auditor may perform such procedures as:

- Making inquiries of appropriate individuals
- Inspecting documents & records
- Observing activities

The auditor is not required to evaluate the effectiveness of controls unless reliance upon them is intended

The auditor is required to document the understanding of the entity's internal control

Common forms of documentation include:

- A **memorandum**, describing the entity's internal control in narrative form
- A **flowchart**, diagramming internal control
- An **internal control questionnaire**, providing management's responses to questions about internal control
- A **decision table**

Flowcharts

Flowcharts diagram the design of internal control

Symbols used:

Manual operation	Process	Decision	Input or output
	Manual Input	Hard copy	Floppy disk
Communication link	On page connector	Computer monitor	Temporary on-line storage

Internal Control Questionnaire

Consists of series of questions asked of management

- Some questions designed to address objectives of internal control
- Other questions designed to address control activities designed to accomplish objectives

Questions designed to require “yes” or “no” answer

- “No” answer generally indicative of weakness in internal control
- Makes identification of weaknesses easier

Assessing Control Risk

Based on the understanding of the design of internal control, the auditor will assess control risk in relation to management's assertions

Control risk may be set at the maximum level for some or all assertions

- The auditor does not intend to rely on internal control in relation to those assertions
- Tests of controls will not be performed

Control risk may be set below maximum for some or all assertions

- The auditor must verify the effectiveness of internal control so that it can be relied upon
- Tests of controls will be performed

Assessing control risk below maximum involves 2 components:

1) Identify controls that will prevent or detect material misstatements in specific assertions
2) Perform tests of control to evaluate the effectiveness of the controls identified

Tests of Controls

Tests of controls include:

- **R**eperformance – repeating procedures performed by client employee's such as recounting inventories or recalculating invoice amounts
- **I**nspection – looking at documentary evidence such as inspecting paid invoices to make certain they have been cancelled to avoid double payment
- **I**nquiry – asking questions of appropriate personnel such as inquiring about the procedure followed when merchandise is received
- **O**bservation – watching client employees as they perform such as observing employees receiving & recording purchases of merchandise to determine if there is proper segregation of duties

The company's president ***raced*** *to* ***Riio*** *(well, I really mean Rio de Janeiro) when it was learned that the assertions were false*

Tests of Controls (continued)

Tests of controls can be used to evaluate the effectiveness of the design of internal control as part of obtaining an understanding

The auditor would

- Inspect documents & reports
- Inquire of appropriate personnel
- Observe the application of specific controls

Tests of controls can also be used to evaluate the operating effectiveness of internal control in the desire to reduce the assessed level of control risk

The auditor would:

- Reperform procedures performed by clients
- Inspect documents & reports
- Inquire of appropriate personnel
- Observe the application of specific controls

Further Reducing the Assessed Level of Control Risk

Since many of the procedures used to understand the design of internal control are also used to support the assessed level of control risk:

- Obtaining an understanding of internal control & supporting the assessed level of control risk are often done simultaneously
- The auditor may determine that additional tests of controls will provide evidence that will further reduce the assessed level of control risk

Auditor may make a decision that:

- Additional tests of controls > reduction in substantive testing – auditor would use assessed level of control risk already established
- Additional tests of controls < reduction in substantive testing – auditor would perform additional tests of control & use the resulting revised assessed level of control risk

Assessed level of control risk is then used to determine maximum level of detection risk that will provide acceptably low audit risk

Documentation

The auditor must document:

- The understanding of the entity's internal control in all circumstances
- The basis for assessing control risk at below maximum for a specific management assertion

The auditor need not document the basis for assessing control risk at the maximum level for a management assertion

	Assess Control Risk at **Below the Maximum** Level	Assess Control Risk **At the Maximum** Level
Document understanding of entity's internal control	Required	Required
Document basis for conclusion concerning control risk	Required	Not required
Perform test of controls to determine effectiveness of policies and procedures	Yes	No
Substantive testing	Yes, but limited if determined that the auditor can rely on internal control	Yes

The Revenue Cycle

Financial Statement Accounts

Various items on the financial statements are affected by the revenue cycle

Net sales – management asserts:

- **R** & O – they have delivered the goods or performed the services to entitle the company to the revenues
- **A** or V – sales were recorded at the appropriate amount
- **C** – all sales & only those sales that occurred during the period are included
- **E** or O – all reported sales occurred during the period
- **D** & P – all sales are properly classified & appropriate disclosures have been made

Revenue Cycle (continued)

Net accounts receivable - management asserts:

- **R** & O – the company is entitled to collect amounts reported as accounts receivable
- **A** or V – accounts receivable are reported at the appropriate amount taking into account uncollectible accounts & expected sales returns & allowances
- **C** – all amounts owed to the company due to sales on account are included in accounts receivable & only those amounts
- **E** or O – all receivables exist
- **D** & P – amounts reported as accounts receivable are properly classified & appropriate disclosures have been made

Revenue Cycle (continued)

Bad debt expense - management asserts:

- **A** or V – bad debt expense has been determined using an appropriate method & reasonable estimates
- **C** – all potential uncollectible amounts have been taken into consideration
- **D** & P – bad debt expense has been properly classified & the policies adopted in calculating it have been disclosed

Cash receipts - management asserts:

- **R** & O – the company is entitled to the amounts collected
- **A** or V – cash receipts have been recorded at the amount collected
- **C** – all amounts & only those amounts collected during the period are included in cash receipts
- **E** or O –all recorded cash receipts occurred during the period

Control Activities

Control Activity	*Management assertion*	*Explanation*
Performance reviews	R & O A or V C E or O	• Compare sales to budget • Compare ratios such as accounts receivable turnover to industry averages
Information processing	R & O A or V C E or O D & P	• Require authorization for sales on credit • Use prenumbered sales invoices • Require shipping documents to accompany invoice before recording sales • Require that sales invoice be footed and crossfooted before recording • Remittance listing prepared for cash received • Bank reconciled timely

Physical controls	R & O C E or O	• Receipts deposited timely • Bonded employees handle cash • Merchandise not shipped without documentation of sale • Customers told to pay by check • Checks restrictively endorsed • Payments mailed to lockbox
Segregation of duties	R & O C E or O	• Authorizing sales on account separate from authorizing credits to accounts receivable • Authorizing sales, recording accounts receivable, & having custody of inventory separate • Custody of cash, recording cash receipts, and reconciling bank account separate • Individuals authorizing sales & bad debt write-offs do not have custody of cash or recording functions

The Purchases & Spending Cycle

Financial Statement Accounts

Various items on the financial statements are affected by the purchases & spending cycle

Net purchases– management asserts:

- **R** & O – merchandise was received creating an obligation to pay
- **A** or V – purchases were recorded at the appropriate amount
- **C** – all purchases & only those purchases that occurred during the period are included
- **E** or O – all reported purchases occurred during the period
- **D** & P – all purchases are properly classified & appropriate disclosures have been made

Purchases and Spending Cycle (continued)

Inventory - management asserts:

- **R** & O – the company owns the merchandise reported as inventory
- **A** or V –inventory is reported under an appropriate cost flow method, taking into account, if appropriate, the lower of cost or market
- **C** – all merchandise owned by the company & only merchandise owned by the company is included in inventory
- **E** or O – all inventory exists
- **D** & P – amounts reported as inventory are properly classified & appropriate disclosures, including the method of accounting for inventory have been made

Purchases and Spending Cycle (continued)

Accounts payable - management asserts:

- **R** & O – the company is obligated to pay amounts reported as accounts payable
- **A** or V – accounts payable is reported at the appropriate amount taking into account expected returns & allowances
- **C** – all amounts owed by the company due to purchases on account are included in accounts payable & only those amounts
- **E** or O – all payables exist
- **D** & P – amounts reported as accounts payable are properly classified & appropriate disclosures have been made

Purchases and Spending Cycle (continued)

Various expenses, prepaid expenses, & accrued expenses - management asserts:

- **R** & O – the company is entitled to future goods & services represented by prepaid expenses & obligated to pay for goods & services already received represented by accrued expenses
- **A** or V – expenses, including prepaid & accrued amounts are reported at the appropriate amounts
- **C** – all expenses incurred & only those incurred by the company during the period are included
- **E** or O – all rights represented by prepaid expenses & all obligations represented by accrued expenses exist
- **D** & P – amounts reported as expenses, prepaid expenses, & accrued expenses are properly classified & appropriate disclosures have been made

Purchases and Spending Cycle (continued)

Cash disbursements- management asserts:

- **R** & O – the company is obligated for the amounts paid
- **A** or V – cash disbursements have been recorded at the amount paid
- **C** – all amounts & only those amounts paid during the period are included in cash disbursements
- **E** or O –all recorded cash disbursements occurred during the period

Control Activities

Control Activity	*Management Assertion*	*Explanation*
Performance reviews	R & O A or V C E or O	• Compare purchases to budget • Compare ratios such as accounts receivable turnover & gross profit percentage to industry averages
Information processing	R & O A or V C E or O D & P	• Require authorization for purchase on account • Use prenumbered purchase requisitions, purchase orders & receiving reports • Check & remittance advice prepared when accompanied by requisition, purchase order, & receiving report • Require that purchase invoice be footed & crossfooted before approving for payment • Bank reconciled timely

Physical controls	R & O C E or O	• Access to unused checks limited • Inventory stored safely with access limited • Checks mailed by treasurer's department upon being signed • Authorized signatures required on checks • Check protector used to prevent unauthorized alteration
Segregation of duties	R & O C E or O	• Authorizing purchases, receiving goods, & recording purchases separate • Authorizing payments, recording payments, & access to checks, & reconciling bank separate • Authority to approve vouchers separate from access to unused purchase orders

Other Cycles

Individual companies will have other cycles, depending on the nature of the company, such as

- Personnel & payroll cycle
- Production & conversion cycle
- Investing & financing cycle

Financial Statement Accounts

Each cycle has an impact on related financial statement accounts

Personnel & payroll cycle

- Payroll expense accounts
- Payroll withholding accounts
- Payroll accruals
- Labor included in manufactured inventories
- Cash disbursements

Production & conversion cycle

- Raw materials, work-in-process, & finished goods inventories
- Cost of goods sold

Investing & financing cycle

- Investments in securities
- Property, plant, & equipment
- Notes & bonds payable
- Stockholders' equity accounts

Internal Control Reports

When auditors learn of weaknesses in a client's internal control, they should generally be communicated to the client

- In an audit engagement, auditor may become aware of weaknesses when obtaining an understanding of internal control or when performing tests of controls
- An auditor may accept a separate engagement to report on internal control

Requirements for Evaluation of Internal Control

	GAAS Audit	Separate Engagement
Why is internal control studied in the engagement?	Determine the nature, timing, and extent of substantive tests	Issue an opinion on management's assertion about internal control
Scope of the study of internal control	Only test controls the auditor is relying upon.	Test all (or most) controls in the affected area.
Use of the auditor's report on internal control	Limited	Not limited unless prepared in conformity with criteria of a regulatory agency
Overall conclusion of auditor for internal control	No opinion; but a list of internal control deficiencies	An opinion on management's assertion about internal control

Reportable Conditions & Material Weaknesses

Reportable condition – significant deficiency in design or operation of internal control

- Could adversely affect company's ability to record, process, summarize, & report financial data
- Should be communicated to audit committee

Examples include:

- Failure to safeguard assets
- Willful wrongdoing by employees or management
- Intentional misapplication of accounting principles
- Absence of appropriate segregation of duties

Material weaknesses – significant reportable condition involving design or operation of one or more internal control components

- Components do not reduce to relatively low level risk that material errors, fraudulent reporting, misappropriation of assets, or illegal acts will not be detected on timely basis
- Not all reportable conditions are material weaknesses

Reports in Connection With Audit

Auditor may become aware of reportable condition during course of audit

- Not obligated to search for reportable conditions
- When discovered, should be reported to audit committee verbally or by written report
- Reporting may occur during or after audit

Report should:

- Indicate purpose of audit & that it was not to provide assurance on internal control
- Include definition of reportable conditions
- Restrict use

Report may not indicate that no reportable conditions were noted

- Could be easily misinterpreted
- May indicate that no material weaknesses were noted

Separate Engagements

May report on management's written assertion about effectiveness of internal control over financial reporting

- Requires examination with more extensive scope than consideration of internal control in financial statement audit
- May report only as of a specific point in time

Management assertions about internal control may relate to:

- Design & operating effectiveness
- Suitability of design
- Design & operating effectiveness based on criteria established by regulatory agency

Assertions may be presented in:

- Separate report to accompany CPA's report
- Representation letter to CPA

Separate Engagements (continued)

Conditions must be met for auditor to examine & report on management's assertion

- Management accepts responsibility for effectiveness of internal control
- Management uses reasonable control criteria to evaluate effectiveness
- Sufficient evidential matter exists to support evaluation
- Management presents its written assertion about the effectiveness

Upon accepting such an engagement, the auditor will

1) Plan the engagement
2) Obtain an understanding of internal control
3) Evaluate the effectiveness of the design
4) Test & evaluate operating effectiveness
5) Form an opinion about management's assertions

Substantive Tests

Evidential Matter

Auditor must gather sufficient competent evidential matter as basis for opinion

Evidence consists of underlying accounting data & corroborating information that will either corroborate or contradict management's assertions

- Underlying accounting data – client's accounting records
- Corroborating information – information supporting underlying data available from client & outside sources

Sufficiency

Relates to quantity of evidence necessary to support opinion

- Evidence likely to be persuasive rather than convincing
- Cost of obtaining evidence should not exceed benefit
- Ultimate decision matter for auditor's judgment

Competency

Based on relevance & validity

- Relevance - must relate to specific management assertion
- Validity – must be of quality that assures evidence is reliable or reasonably free from error & bias & faithfully represents what it purports to

Reliability

Reliability of evidential matter largely dependent on circumstances under which it was obtained

- Evidence obtained from independent sources is more reliable than evidence obtained from within the entity
- Effective internal control results in more reliable accounting data & financial statements
- Auditor's personal knowledge more persuasive than information obtained indirectly

Evidential matter can be compared from most reliable to least reliable

- Auditor developed – evidence resulting from auditor's direct personal knowledge obtained through physical examination, observation, computation, & inspection
- Independent – evidence obtained from sources outside of the entity
- Externally developed – evidence prepared by sources outside of the entity & obtained through the client
- Internally developed – evidence prepared by the entity

Nature, Timing, & Extent of Evidential Matter

Audit risk model used to determine acceptable level of detection risk

- Understanding of design of internal control used to assess level of control risk
- Assessed level of control risk, along with inherent risk, used in audit risk model to determine level of detection risk that will provide acceptable level of audit risk
- Resulting acceptable level of detection risk may be high – less convincing evidence is required
- Resulting acceptable level of detection risk may be low – more convincing evidence is required

Effects of Substantive Tests on Detection Risk

	Lower Detection Risk	Higher Detection Risk
General Effective ness	More effective substantive tests	Less effective substantive tests
Nature	Gather evidential matter that is more competent	Gather evidential matter that is less competent
Timing	Gather evidence after year-end	Gather evidence prior to year-end (interim)
Extent	Verify a larger number of transactions or components of the account balance	Verify a smaller number of transactions or components of the account balance

Timing of Audit Procedures

Audit procedures may be performed at interim dates

Substantive testing performed before the balance sheet date:

- Increase risk that misstatements existing at balance sheet date will not be detected
- Referred to as **incremental audit risk**
- Incremental audit risk increases as time between tests & year end is greater

Before performing substantive tests on an interim date, the auditor should consider:

- Effectiveness of internal control
- Changing business conditions that may affect management's judgment in remaining period
- Whether year end balances of accounts being tested are reasonably predictable

Tests should be performed at year-end to cover the remaining period

Gathering Evidence

Audit program is auditor's plan for gathering evidence

- Auditor establishes audit objectives
- Designs steps to accomplish audit objectives
- Write audit program

Developing the Audit Program

Auditor will use a 4-step process

1) Consider management's assertion to be corroborated or contradicted
    - **R**ights & obligations
    - **A**llocation or valuation
    - **C**ompleteness
    - **E**xistence or occurrence
    - **D**isclosure & presentation
2) Determine the level of assurance needed in regard to the assertion
3) Evaluate evidence available
4) Design substantive test that will achieve audit objective of corroborating specific management assertion

Types of Substantive Tests

Although there are a wide variety of substantive tests that can be employed, they can be classified in the following categories:

- **I**nquiries of management regarding matters of concern
- **C**onfirmation from third parties of information incorporated in management's assertion
- **C**omparison of information incorporated in management's assertion to other related information
- **O**bservation of assets or procedures
- **R**ecalculation of information developed by the client
- **E**xamination of documents supporting management's assertion
- **A**nalytical procedures

__I C COREA__ (I see Korea) every time I audit my manufacturing client

Substantive tests may be test of details or analytical procedures

Tests of details are designed to corroborate or contradict specific management assertions

- Tests of details include inquiries, confirmation, comparison, observation, recalculation, and examination
- The result of the test will be information that either agrees with or does not agree with information presented or disclosed in the financial statements

Some information cannot be directly corroborated or contradicted

- Analytical procedures provide evidence as to the reasonableness of management's assertions
- Analytical procedures involve comparing information in the financial statements to expectations to evaluate the relationships
- Analytical procedures may involve financial & nonfinancial data

Analytical Procedures

Analytical procedures (APs) involving comparing amounts recorded in the financial statements or ratios derived from those amounts to expectations

Expectations may be based on:

- Prior financial information
- Budgeted, forecasted, or otherwise anticipated results
- Relationships among elements of the current period's financial statements
- Industry averages
- Relationship between financial & nonfinancial information

APs are used in various stages of the audit

- Planning – APs are used in obtaining an understanding of the client, its business, & its industry (required)
- Substantive testing – APs are used as a substantive test in determining if information incorporated in specific management assertions is reasonable (recommended)
- Overall review – APs are used to determine if conclusions reached are reasonable (required)

Planning

APs can be used in planning to:

- Enhance the auditor's understanding of the client's business & industry
- Enhance the auditor's understanding of transactions & events occurring since the previous audit
- Identify areas representing risks that are relevant to the audit

Information resulting APs can alert auditor as to:

- Unusual transactions & events
- Ratios & trends that might affect the financial statements, particularly those involving income statement accounts

APs assist auditor in planning nature, timing, & extent of audit procedures

APs Used in Substantive Testing

Based on level of assurance needed in relation to a specific management assertion:

- APs alone may be sufficient
- APs may be used in conjunction with tests of detail
- APs may not be appropriate

When applying APs to substantive testing

1) Evaluate nature of assertion to determine if APs are appropriate & if use of APs will be efficient & effective
2) Evaluate whether plausible relationship exists & whether relationship is predictable
3) Determine if information is available & evaluate reliability of available information
4) Determine if expectation is sufficiently precise to provide meaningful conclusions
   - When information is expected to precisely match anticipated information, differences very useful in identifying potential misstatements
   - When information is not expected to precisely match anticipated information, differences may be result of variety of causes
5) Investigate & evaluate differences

Overall Review

Used to evaluate conclusions drawn as a result of audit

Involves:

- Reading financial statements & notes
- Considering adequacy of evidence gathered
- Considering unusual or unexpected items not previously identified

May result in determination that additional evidence is required

Ratios Used in APs

1) Liquidity ratios

   Current ratio = current assets ÷ current liabilities

   Quick or acid test ratio = quick or liquid assets ÷ current liabilities

   Quick or liquid assets are cash & cash equivalents, current investments in marketable securities, & net accounts receivable

2) Activity ratios

   Accounts receivable turnover = net credit sales ÷ average net accounts receivable

   Inventory turnover = cost of goods sold ÷ average inventory

   Asset turnover = net sales ÷ average total assets

3) Profitability ratios

   Gross margin percentage = gross margin ÷ sales

   Net operating margin percentage = operating income ÷ sales

4) Coverage ratios

   Times interest earned = income before interest & taxes ÷ interest expense

   Debt to equity percentage = total debt ÷ total equity

Auditing Specific Accounts

Using Management Assertions to Develop Audit Programs

For each management assertion, the auditor selects auditing procedures from a variety of procedures available

- Procedures include:

    Inquiry
    Confirmation
    Comparison
    Observation
    Recalculation
    Examination
    Analytical procedures

- Not all procedures will apply to each assertion

What is Management Asserting?	*Which Substantive Procedures Will Corroborate or Contradict Assertion?*
R & O	**I**nquiry **C**onfirmation **C**omparison **O**bservation **R**ecalculation **E**xamination **A**nalytical procedures
A or V	**I**nquiry **C**onfirmation **C**omparison **O**bservation **R**ecalculation **E**xamination **A**nalytical procedures

What is Management Asserting?	***Which Substantive Procedures Will Corroborate or Contradict Assertion?***
C	**I**nquiry **C**onfirmation **C**omparison **O**bservation **R**ecalculation **E**xamination **A**nalytical procedures
E or O	**I**nquiry **C**onfirmation **C**omparison **O**bservation **R**ecalculation **E**xamination **A**nalytical procedures

What is Management Asserting?	***Which Substantive Procedures Will Corroborate or Contradict Assertion?***
D & P	**I**nquiry **C**onfirmation **C**omparison **O**bservation **R**ecalculation **E**xamination **A**nalytical procedures

Test of Balances Approach

Accounts can be audited using either a test of balances approach or a test of transactions approach

The test of balances approach is more appropriate when:

- The number of transactions is relatively high
- The dollar amount per transaction is relatively low
- The acceptable level of detection risk is high

Accounts for which this approach is appropriate include cash, accounts receivable & sales, inventory, & accounts payable

This approach involves 3 steps:

1) Identify the components that make up the account balance
2) Select the components to be verified
3) Verify the components through the use of substantive procedures

Auditing Cash

Various procedures used to audit cash

- Auditor would desire high level of assurance in relation to cash
- The acceptable level of detection risk for cash would be relatively low
- Auditor will generally use a test of balances approach

AICPA Standard Bank Confirmation

- Form developed by AICPA used in all financial statement audits
- Mailed to each bank in which client has or had accounts
- Requests information regarding balances, loans, & restrictions on cash balances

R & O – management asserts that cash reported on balance sheet belongs to client

- Inquire of management if there are restrictions on cash
- Confirm with bank, using Standard AICPA Bank Confirmation, that there are no restrictions on cash such as compensating balances

A or V – management asserts that cash is reported on balance sheet in correct amount

- Confirm balance per bank using Standard AICPA Bank Confirmation
- Compare amount on confirmation to amount on bank reconciliation
- Compare ending balance on bank reconciliation to schedule of cash balances
- Compare total amount from schedule of cash balances to amount reported on balance sheet
- Observe counts of cash on hand
- Recalculate amounts on bank reconciliation
- Examine interbank transfer schedule to verify absence of kiting

C – management asserts that cash reported on balance sheet represents all of the company's cash & that all transactions involving cash were recorded in the appropriate period

- Confirm that reconciling items are reported in appropriate period using bank cutoff statement
- Compare deposits in transit on bank reconciliation to deposits reported in the cutoff statement
- Compare outstanding checks on bank reconciliation to checks cleared in the cutoff statement

E or O – management asserts that cash reported on the balance sheet actually exists

- Confirm bank deposits using AICPA Standard Bank Confirmation
- Confirm certificates of deposit & other cash equivalents held by bank or others
- Observe cash on hand
- Examine certificates of deposit & other cash equivalents on hand

D & P – Management asserts that cash & cash equivalents are properly classified & any pertinent information is adequately disclosed

- Inquire of management about compensating balances or other restrictions on cash
- Confirm restrictions on cash using AICPA Standard Bank Confirmation
- Examine financial statements & disclosures to make certain that cash is properly presented & disclosed

Auditing Accounts Receivable & Sales

A common tool used in auditing accounts receivable is the accounts receivable confirmation

- The auditor sends the confirmation to the client's customer
- The customer corroborates or contradicts the amount the client indicates is owed by the customer

Positive confirmations – require a response from the customer indicating agreement or disagreement with amount indicated by the client

Used when:

- Relatively low number of accounts with relatively high balances
- Acceptable detection risk is relatively low
- Customer may be unlikely to respond

Negative confirmations – require a response only if customer disagrees with balance

Used when:

- Relatively high number of accounts with relatively low balances
- Acceptable detection risk is relatively high
- Customer is more likely to respond

R & O – management asserts that company is entitled to the amounts reported as accounts receivable

- Inquire of management if accounts receivable have been pledged, assigned, or sold
- Examine loan agreements for indications of accounts receivable financing
- Examine minutes of meetings of board of directors for indications of accounts receivable financing

A or V – management asserts that accounts receivable is reported at its net realizable value

- Inquire of management as to policies for collecting & writing off delinquent accounts
- Confirm balances in accounts receivable using positive or negative confirmations
- Compare amounts reported on confirmations to accounts receivable schedule
- Compare total of accounts receivable schedule to amount reported on balance sheet
- Recalculate balances of the allowance for uncollectible accounts & allowances for sales discounts & sales returns & allowances
- Examine the aged analysis to determine if allowances are reasonable
- Examine subsequent collections & shipping documents for receivables for which positive confirmations were not returned
- Apply analytical procedures to determine if accounts receivable balance is reasonable in relation to sales & other factors

C – management asserts that all amounts owed to the company resulting from sales on account are included in accounts receivable & that all transactions related to sales & accounts receivable were recorded in the appropriate period

- Compare shipping documents to amounts recorded as sales to determine if all sales were recorded
- Examine numerical sequence of prenumbered shipping documents & invoices to make certain that all numbers are accounted for
- Examine shipping logs & shipping documents for shipments at or near year-end to verify appropriate cutoff

E or O – management asserts that amounts reported as accounts receivable exist & reported sales transactions actually occurred

- Confirm amounts reported in accounts receivable using positive or negative confirmations
- Compare recorded sales to invoices & shipping documents to determine that goods were sold & shipped
- Compare deposits to dates receipts were recorded to verify absence of lapping
- Examine subsequent collections & shipping documents for receivables for which positive confirmations were not returned

D & P – management asserts that amounts reported as sales & accounts receivable are properly classified on the financial statements & any pertinent information is adequately disclosed

- Inquire of management as to whether any accounts receivable are pledged as collateral for a loan
- Ascertain whether receivables from related parties are identified for disclosure purposes
- Examine accounts receivable listing to verify that loans from officers & other amounts are not included
- Examine loan agreements for indication of pledging of receivables
- Examine financial statements & disclosures to make certain that accounts receivable is properly presented & disclosed
- Examine minutes of directors meetings for indications of accounts receivable financing

Auditing Inventory

R & O – management asserts that the company owns the inventory reported & that it has not been pledged as collateral for a loan

- Inquire of management if inventory is being held on consignment or has been pledged as security
- Examine loan agreements to determine if inventory is pledged as security
- Examine purchase invoices to verify that inventory is owned rather than held on consignment
- Examine minutes of directors meetings for indications of inventory financing

A or V – management asserts that inventory is properly reported using an appropriate inventory valuation method & at the lower of cost or market when appropriate

- Inquire as to the inventory valuation method in use
- Compare amounts resulting from test counts to amounts reported on inventory schedules
- Compare inventory costs to amounts on purchase invoices
- Compare totals from inventory schedules to amounts reported on balance sheet
- Compare amounts from cost sheets to amounts reported for manufactured inventory
- Observe counts of inventory to verify accuracy
- Recalculate selected amounts & totals on inventory schedules using costs & quantities to verify accuracy
- Examine cost sheets for proper handling of direct materials, direct labor, & application of overhead
- Examine inventory schedules to verify proper application of inventory cost method
- Apply analytical procedures to determine if inventory is reasonable in relation to cost of sales & other related items

C – management asserts that all inventory owned by the company is included in the reported balance & that all transactions related to inventory are recorded in the appropriate period

- Inquire of management as to inventories stored outside the entity
- Confirm inventories held by consignees, warehouses, & others outside the entity
- Compare amounts from test counts to inventory schedules
- Compare totals of inventory schedules to amount reported on balance sheet
- Examine shipping documents for goods in transit to determine if appropriately included or excluded from inventory

E or O – management asserts that all inventory that is reported in the financial statements actually exists

- Confirm inventories held by consignees, public warehouses, & others outside the entity
- Observe the counting of inventory
- Examine shipping documents for inventory in transit

D & P – management asserts that amounts reported as inventory in the financial statements is properly classified & any pertinent information has been adequately disclosed

- Inquire of management if inventory is pledged as security for a loan
- Examine loan agreements for indication of financing of inventory
- Examine financial statements & disclosures to make certain that inventory is properly presented & components & inventory valuation method are properly disclosed
- Examine minutes of directors meetings for indications of inventory financing

Auditing Accounts Payable & Purchases

R & O – management asserts that the company is obligated to pay accounts payable

- Compare amounts showing as payable to vendors' invoices, receiving reports, & purchase orders to verify that payables are for goods ordered & received
- Examine vendors' invoices, receiving reports, & purchase orders

A & V – management asserts that accounts payable is reported at the amount that the company is obligated to pay

- Confirm amounts reported as payables with vendors
- Compare amounts reported as payables to vendors' invoices, receiving reports, & purchase orders
- Compare amount on schedule of accounts payable to amount reported on financial statements
- Recalculate totals of accounts payable schedule
- Apply analytical procedures to determine if relationships between accounts payable & purchases, inventory, cost of goods sold, & other items are reasonable

C – management asserts that all amounts owed to vendors for purchases on account are included in accounts payable & that all transactions related to accounts payable & purchases are reported in the appropriate period

- Confirm with vendors that balances are complete
- Confirm with vendors with zero balances to determine if amounts are owed
- Compare receiving reports to vendors' invoices & amounts recorded in accounts payable
- Examine payments made shortly after year end to determine if goods or services were received before year end

E or O – management asserts that the obligation to pay accounts payable exists & that all purchase transactions did occur

- Confirm accounts payable with vendors
- Compare amounts reported in accounts payable to vendors' invoices, receiving reports, & purchase orders
- Examine payments after year end to verify obligation existing at year end

D & P –management asserts that amounts reported as accounts payable are properly classified on the financial statements & any pertinent information is adequately disclosed

- Examine financial statements & disclosures to make certain that accounts receivable is properly presented & disclosed
- Ascertain whether payables to related parties are identified for disclosure purposes

Test of Transactions Approach

The test of transactions approach is more appropriate when:

- The number of transactions is relatively low
- The dollar amount per transaction is relatively high
- The acceptable level of detection risk is low

Accounts for which this approach is appropriate include long-term investments & investments in marketable securities; property, plant, & equipment; long-term debt; & equity

This approach involves 4 steps:

1) Verify account's beginning balance from prior-year information
2) Test transactions occurring during the current period through the use of substantive procedures
3) Verify resulting ending balance in account
4) Determine if ending balance is in need of adjustment due to impairment, change in market value, or other factor
5) Perform other procedures for management assertions not already addressed

Auditing Investments & Investment Income

1) Verify account's beginning balance from prior-year information
   - Compare beginning balance in investment accounts to amounts reported on previous period's balance sheet (A or V)
2) Test transactions occurring during the current period through the use of substantive procedures
   - Inquire of management about acquisitions & disposals of investments during period (R & O, C, E or O)
   - Inquire of management about means of determining value of investments other than marketable securities (A or V)
   - Confirm purchases or sales where documents are not in evidence (R & O, C, E or O)
   - Compare amounts reported as investment income to amounts published in investment periodicals (A or V, C, E or O)
   - Compare amounts reported as investment income to amounts deposited (A or V, C, E or O)
   - Compare amount recorded as cost of investment to documents from brokers, partnership agreements, & joint venture agreements (A or V)
   - Recalculate amortization of discount or premium & verify proper recording (A or V)

Auditing Investments and Investment Income (continued)

- Recalculate gains & losses on sales based on documents from brokers or amounts deposited & carrying value of investment (A & V)
- Examine documents from brokers & canceled checks to verify acquisitions (R & O, A or V, E or O)
- Examine audited financial statements of investees accounted for under equity method for verifying of amount reported as income (A or V)
- Examine minutes of directors meetings for indications of authorization of acquisitions & disposals of investments (C)
- Apply analytical procedures to verify reasonableness of amount reported as interest income (A or V, C)

3) Verify resulting ending balance in account
   - Recalculate ending balance based on beginning balance & transactions during the period (A or V)

Auditing Investments & Investment Income (continued)

4) Determine if ending balance is in need of adjustment due to impairment, change in market value, or other factor
   - Inquire of management if any long-term investments or investments in marketable securities classified as available for sale have experienced a nontemporary decline in value (A or V, D & P)
   - Confirm investments held by brokers or other outside parties to verify they are still in existence & owned by the company (R & O, C, E or O)
   - Compare carrying value of investments to market values to verify that investments are carried at lower of cost or market when appropriate (A or V, D & P)
   - Examine stock certificates, bonds, partnership agreements, or joint venture agreements to verify that investments exist (E or O)

5) Perform other procedures for management assertions not already addressed
   - Inquire of management as to its intention for holding investments to verify classification (D & P)
   - Examine financial statements & disclosures to make certain that investments are properly presented & disclosed (D & P)

Auditing Property, Plant, & Equipment

1) Verify account's beginning balance from prior-year information
   - Compare beginning balance in property, plant, & equipment accounts to amounts reported on previous period's balance sheet (A or V)
2) Test transactions occurring during the current period through the use of substantive procedures
   - Inquire of management about acquisitions & disposals of property, plant, & equipment during period (R & O, C, E or O)
   - Inquire of management about methods, lives, & salvage values used to calculate depreciation (A or V)
   - Confirm purchases or sales where documents are not in evidence (R & O, C, E or O)
   - Compare amount recorded as cost of property, plant, & equipment to purchase documents & cancelled checks (A or V)
   - Recalculate costs to be capitalized for delivery, installation, or preparation of property, plant, & equipment for use (A or V, C)
   - Recalculate depreciation expense & verify proper recording (A or V)

Auditing Property, Plant, & Equipment (continued)

- Recalculate gains & losses on sales based on amounts deposited & carrying value of property, plant, & equipment (A & V)
- Examine invoices & canceled checks to verify acquisitions (R & O, A or V, E or O)
- Examine minutes of directors meetings for indications of authorization of acquisitions & disposals of property, plant, & equipment (C)

3) Verify resulting ending balance in account
   - Recalculate ending balance based on beginning balance & transactions during the period (A or V)

4) Determine if ending balance is in need of adjustment due to impairment, change in market value, or other factor
   - Inquire of management if any impairments have occurred affecting property, plant, & equipment (A or V, D & P)
   - Examine property, plant, & equipment to verify that they exist (E or O)

Auditing Property, Plant, & Equipment (continued)

5) Perform other procedures for management assertions not already addressed

   - Examine financial statements & disclosures to make certain that property, plant, & equipment is properly presented & disclosed, that methods used for determining depreciation are disclosed, & that amount of depreciation recognized for the period is disclosed (D & P)

Auditing Long-Term Debt & Interest Expense

1) Verify account's beginning balance from prior-year information
   - Compare beginning balance in long-term debt accounts to amounts reported on previous period's balance sheet (A or V)

2) Test transactions occurring during the current period through the use of substantive procedures
   - Inquire of management about issuance & retirements of long-term debt during period (R & O, C, E or O)
   - Compare amounts reported as interest expense to amounts disbursed (A or V, E or O)
   - Compare amount recorded as proceeds from issuance to confirmations from underwriters & amounts deposited (A or V, E or O)
   - Compare amounts reported in cash receipts journal to amounts recorded as initial carrying value of long-term debt (A or V, C)
   - Recalculate amortization of discount or premium & verify proper recording (A or V)
   - Recalculate gains & losses on early retirements (A & V)
   - Examine documents from underwriters & trustees to verify issuances (R & O, A or V, E or O)

Auditing Long-Term Debt & Interest Expense (continued)

- Examine minutes of directors meetings for indications of authorization of issuances & retirements of long-term debt (C)
- Apply analytical procedures to verify reasonableness of amount reported as interest expense (A or V, C)

3) Verify resulting ending balance in account
   - Recalculate ending balance based on beginning balance & transactions during the period (A or V)

Auditing Long-Term Debt & Interest Expense (continued)

4) Determine if ending balance is in need of adjustment due to impairment, change in market value, or other factor
   - Confirm obligations with trustees or other outside parties to verify there are no unrecorded liabilities (R & O, C, E or O)
   - Confirm obligations with creditors to determine that they are the obligations of the company (R & O, E or O)
   - Examine bond agreements & long-term notes to verify that long-term liabilities exist (E or O)
   - Examine documents relating to renewal or refinancing of debt after balance date to support classification as long-term (D & P)

5) Perform other procedures for management assertions not already addressed
   - Inquire of management as to its intention for retiring debt prior to maturity (D & P)
   - Examine financial statements & disclosures to make certain that long-term debt is properly presented & disclosed & that gains & losses on early retirement are reported as extraordinary items (D & P)
   - Examine documents to verify that company is complying with debt covenants (D & P)

Auditing Equity

1) Verify account's beginning balance from prior-year information
    - Compare beginning balance in long-term debt accounts to amounts reported on previous period's balance sheet (A or V)
2) Test transactions occurring during the current period through the use of substantive procedures
    - Inquire of management about issuance & retirements of equity securities during period (R & O, C, E or O)
    - Compare amounts reported as dividends to amounts disbursed (A or V, E or O)
    - Compare amount recorded as proceeds from issuance to confirmations from underwriters & deposits (A or V, E or O)
    - Compare amounts reported in cash receipts journal to amounts recorded as proceeds from issuance of debt securities (A or V, C)
    - Examine documents from underwriters & stock transfer agents to verify issuances & repurchases of stock (R & O, A or V, E or O)
    - Verify changes in Accumulated Other Comprehensive Income amounts (A or V, D & P)
    - Examine minutes of directors meetings for indications of authorization of dividends & issuances & retirements of equity securities (C)

Auditing Equity (continued)

3) Verify resulting ending balance in account
   - Recalculate ending balance based on beginning balance & transactions during the period (A or V)

4) Determine if ending balance is in need of adjustment due to impairment, change in market value, or other factor

5) Perform other procedures for management assertions not already addressed
   - Inquire of management as to its intention for retiring debt prior to maturity (D & P)
   - Examine financial statements & disclosures to make certain that long-term debt is properly presented & disclosed & that gains & losses on early retirement are reported as extraordinary items (D & P)
   - Examine employee stock purchase plans to analyze terms (D & P)
   - Examine appropriate laws to determine if there are restrictions on retained earnings (D & P)
   - Examine documents to verify that company is complying with debt covenants

Issues Related to Substantive Testing

Accounting Estimates

Auditor responsible for reasonableness of estimates used in determining the amounts of elements of the financial statements

When evaluating reasonableness, the auditor concentrates on assumptions or factors:

- Significant to the estimate
- Sensitive to variation
- Apparent deviations from historical patterns
- Subjective & susceptible to bias or misstatement

The auditor should understand how management develops estimates & obtain satisfaction through:

- Reviewing & testing the process used by management (recalculation)
- Developing an independent expectation of the estimate to compare to management's amount (analytical procedures)
- Review subsequent events or transactions prior to completing fieldwork to verify the estimate (comparison)

Internal Auditors

Internal auditors may have an effect on the audit in 2 separate respects

- The internal audit function may affect the nature, timing, & extent of audit procedures necessary to form a basis for an opinion on the financial statements
- The internal auditors may provide direct assistance in the performance of the audit

The impact of an internal audit function on the nature, timing, & extent of audit procedures will depend on the competence & objectivity of the internal auditors

- Competence relates to their qualifications
- Objectivity relates to the organizational level to which they report

Internal auditors may have an effect on:

- Procedures performed in obtaining an understanding of internal control
- Procedures performed in assessing the risk of material misstatement
- Substantive procedures performed

Internal Auditors (continued)

Regardless of the use of internal auditors, certain judgments remain the responsibility of the independent auditor:

- Assessments of inherent & control risks
- Materiality
- Sufficiency of tests performed
- Evaluation of significant estimates
- Other matters affecting the auditor's report

The effect of the work of the independent auditor depends on the degree to which an item is susceptible to risk of material misstatement

- When the risk is relatively high, the work of the internal auditors will not eliminate the independent auditor's need to test the assertions
- When the risk is relatively low, the work of the internal auditors may be sufficient to reduce audit risk to an acceptable level avoiding the need for the independent auditor to test the assertions directly

Specialists

Auditors may rely on the work of specialists to:

- Value assets
- Determine the physical characteristics of inventories
- Determine amounts derived through specialized techniques
- Interpret technical requirements, regulations, or agreements

Before relying on the work of a specialist, the auditor should:

- Evaluate the qualifications of the specialist
- Understand the nature of the work to be performed by the specialist
- Evaluate the relationship of the specialist to the client

In evaluating the findings of the specialist, the auditor should:

- Understand the methods used & assumptions made
- Test data provided to the specialist
- Evaluate whether the findings support the related assertions

Specialists (continued)

The use of a specialist will not generally have an effect on the auditor's report

- The auditor may add explanatory language to the standard report as a result of the findings of the specialist
- The auditor may decide to modify the opinion if the findings of the specialist do not corroborate the related assertions

The use of a specialist will only be referred to in the audit report if the findings of the specialist resulted in a modification of the report

Litigation, Claims & Assessments

Management is responsible for identifying, evaluating, & accounting for litigation, claims, & assessments (l, c, & a)

Management asserts that all l, c, & a have been appropriately considered & are properly reflected in the financial statements & related disclosures

The auditor obtains evidence relating to:

- The existence of conditions indicating an uncertainty arising from l, c, & a
- The period in which the cause for the uncertainty occurred
- The probability of an unfavorable outcome
- The amount or range of potential loss

Litigation, Claims, & Assessments (continued)

The auditor's procedures will include:

- Inquire of management policies & procedures for identifying, evaluating, & accounting for l, c, & a
- Obtain from management a description and evaluation of l, c, & a existing at the balance sheet date
- Examine documents, including correspondence & invoices from lawyers concerning l, c, & a
- Obtain written assurance from management that all unasserted claims that are probable of assertion have been disclosed
- Obtain letter from client's attorney regarding l, c, & a

Client sends letter to attorney requesting corroboration of information supplied by management regarding l, c, & a

Included in letter:

- Identification of company & date of audit
- List prepared by management describing & evaluating pending or threatened l, c, & a
- List prepared by management describing & evaluating unasserted claims & assessments management considers probable of assertion
- Request that lawyer furnish information regarding pending or threatened l, c, & a
- Request that lawyer comment on views differing from those of management related to l, c, & a
- Statement that lawyer will advise & consult with client regarding disclosure of unasserted possible claims or assessments
- Request that lawyer identify nature of & reasons for limitations on response to inquiry

The lawyer will respond with:

- Description of pending l, c, & a including progress to date and intended actions
- Evaluation of probability of unfavorable outcome & estimate of range of loss
- Omissions, if any, of pending or threatened l, c, & a from list prepared by client

Lawyer's refusal to respond represents a scope limitation

Related Parties

Audit procedures should be performed to identify & evaluate the disclosure of related party transactions

In performing the audit, transactions may come to the auditor's attention indicating the existence of related parties

- Borrowing or lending at no interest or at rates significantly different from market rates
- Sales of real estate at prices significantly different from appraised values
- Exchanges of similar property in nonmonetary transactions
- Loans with no scheduled terms

Procedures the auditor will apply include:

- Examine minutes of board meetings
- Examine transactions with major customers, supplier, borrowers, & lenders for indications of relationship
- Examine large, unusual, or nonrecurring transactions at or near year end
- Examine confirmations of loans receivable & payable for guarantees

Related Parties (continued)

If related party transactions are identified, auditor should

- Obtain understanding of business purpose of transaction
- Examine invoices, agreements, & contracts
- Determine whether the directors have approved the transaction
- Evaluate disclosures for reasonableness

Management Representations

The auditor must obtain written representations from management indicating:

- **I**nformation & data was available to the auditor during the examination
- **R**esponsibility for the financial statements rests with management
- **E**rrors, fraud, & material litigation that are known at year end have been communicated
- **S**ubsequent events that may effect carrying values have been communicated
- **P**lans of the company that may effect carrying values have been communicated
- **O**ral information provided to the auditor was accurate & complete
- **N**oncompliance with laws & regulations that are known at year end have been communicated
- **D**isclosure of major transactions, events, or circumstances affecting the client at year end has been made

When the auditor asks me a question, ***I RESPOND***

Management Representations (continued)

Written representations of management are addressed to the auditor:

- Dated as of the date of the auditor's report
- Generally signed by chief executive officer & chief financial officer

When management will not supply a written representation letter

- Constitutes a scope limitation
- Auditor precluded from issuing unqualified opinion
- May affect auditor's attitude toward other information supplied by management

Working Papers

Working papers are documentation of work performed

- Demonstrate auditor's adherence to the standards of field work
- Assist the auditor in conducting & supervising the audit

Working papers are maintained in permanent files & current files

Permanent files relate to the company & contain information with long-term significance

They are of ongoing interest in any period under audit & often include:

- Debt agreements
- Pension contracts
- Articles of incorporation
- Flowcharts of internal control
- Bond indenture agreements
- Lease agreements
- Analyses of capital stock & owners' equity accounts

Working Papers (continued)

Current files relate specifically to the current period's audit

They often include:

- Reconciliation of accounting records to financial statements or other information reported on
- Lead schedules reflecting major components of amounts in the financial statements
- Supporting schedules providing detail making up major components
- Documentation of substantive procedures performed providing evidence corroborating or contradicting management's assertions
- The attorney's letter & management's representation letter
- Audit programs

Working papers are the property of the auditor & should be maintained for a reasonable period

Working papers may be in the form of electronic files

Responsibilities in an Information Technology Environment

Audit objectives are the same when financial records are manual or developed in an information technology (IT) environment.

In an IT environment, the auditor should consider:

- Client use of computers in significant accounting applications
- Complexity of the entity's computer operations
- Organizational structure of computer processing activities
- Availability of data
- Use of computer assisted audit techniques (CAATS) for audit procedures

Electronic Commerce

Electronic commerce using **electronic data interchange** or **EDI** adds to the complexity of auditing. EDI enables:

- Communication without the use of paper
- Electronic funds transfers and sales over the Internet
- Simplification of the recording process using scanning devices
- Sending information to trading partners as transactions occur

EDI transactions are formatted using strict standards that have been agreed to worldwide, often requiring companies to acquire translation software

Risks of E-Commerce

Electronic commerce increases the risk of improper use of information. Controls might include:

- Data encryption
- Controls to prevent electronic eavesdropping

There is also the risk of improper distribution of transactions with information being electronically transmitted to an inappropriate company. Controls might include

- Routing verification procedures
- Message acknowledgement procedures

The reduction in the paper audit trail associated with EDI creates special challenges to the auditor.

- Detection risk may not be sufficiently reduced through substantive testing
- Control risk must be reduced adequately to achieve an acceptable level of audit risk
- Controls must be built into the system to insure the validity of information captured

Networks

In a computer network, computers are connected to one another to enable sharing of peripheral devices, sharing data and programs stored on a **file server**, and communicating with one another.

Networks allow various user departments to share information files maintained in **databases**. Databases should:

- Provide departments with information that is appropriate
- Prevent access to inappropriate information

A company may create its own **value added network** or **VAN**.

- A **local area networks** (**LAN**) is used when computers are physically near to one another
- A **wide area network** (**WAN**) uses high-speed, long distance communications networks or satellites to connect computers that are not near to one another

The Internet

The **Internet** is a worldwide network that allows virtually any computer system to link to it by way of an electronic gateway. The Internet facilitates data communication services including:

- Remote login
- File transfer
- Electronic mail
- Newsgroups

Intranets use Internet technology in closed networks

Extranets use Internet technology to link businesses with suppliers, customers, and others

Networks are part of a decentralized processing system applying **distributed data processing**. Users share programs, peripheral devices, and data.

In **client/server computing**, smaller programs are distributed to the workstations enabling the user to communicate with the network, referred to as front-end processing.

In **end user computing**, a user department generates and uses its own information.

Networks and Control Risk

To minimize control risk, a network should have some form of security that limits access to certain files to authorized individuals.

- Certain individuals may have read only access to files
- Others will be authorized to alter the data in the files

A tool for establishing such security is a **firewall**, which prevents unauthorized users from accessing data

Hardware

Hardware is the actual electronic equipment. Common components include:

- **Central Processing Unit** or **CPU** – The principal hardware component that processes programs
- **Memory** – The internal storage space or **online storage**, often referred to as **random access memory** or **RAM**
- **Offline Storage** –Devices used to store data or programs externally, including floppy disks, magnetic tape, digital video disks (DVDs), and compact disks (CDs)
- **File Server** – A computer with a large internal memory used to store programs and data that can be accessed by all workstations in the network
- **Input and Output Devices** – Devices that allow for communication between the computer and users and for the storage of data such as a terminal with a screen and a keyboard, scanners, microphones, wireless hand-held units, barcode readers, point of sale registers, optical character readers, mark sense readers, light guns, printers, speakers, floppy disk drives, CD and DVD drives, magnetic tape drives, and magnetic disk drives

Software

Software is either system software or application software.

- **System software** is made up of the programs that run the system and direct its operations, comprised of the operating system and utility programs
- **Utility** programs are used for sorts, merges, and other routine functions to maintain and improve the efficiency of a computer system
- Specialized **security software** is a type of utility program used to control access to the computer or its files

The Accounting Process In An IT Environment

The two primary approaches to the processing of data are batch processing and online processing.

- **Batch processing** - Input data is collected over a period of time and processed periodically
- **Online processing** - Individuals originating transactions process them from remote locations in a batch, similar to batch processing, or immediately in an **online, real time system**

Online, real time systems update accounting records immediately as transactions occur, but result in significant changes in internal control.

- Source documents are often not available to support input into the computer
- The audit trail is usually significantly reduced requiring controls programmed into the computer

Organization of an IT Environment

Organization of the IT function is largely dependent on the size of the company and the number of employees involved

- Larger companies will have a separate IT department
- Others will have many IT functions performed by employees in the accounting department and end users

One characteristic of an IT environment is a reduction in the segregation of duties. Although this might appear to create a potential problem:

- A computer has no incentive to conceal its errors
- Functions can often be combined in an IT environment without weakening internal control

Organization in a Segregated Department

In a well-staffed IT department, systems, operations, and other technical services would be segregated. Each of these segments would be under the supervision of the information systems manager who might report to the president of the company, one of the vice presidents, or the controller.

Systems might include:

- A **systems analyst** designs the information system using systems flowcharts and other tools and prepares specifications for applications programmers.
- An **application programmer** writes, tests, and debugs programs that will be used in the system. The programmer also develops instructions for operators to follow when running the programs.
- A **database administrator** plans and administers the database to make certain that only appropriate individuals have access to information in it.

Operations might include data entry, computer operations, program and file librarians, and data control.

- A **data entry clerk** converts data into computer readable form.
- A **computer operator** runs the programs on the computer.
- **Program and file librarians** are responsible for the custody of computer programs, master files, transaction files, and other records.
- **Data control** is responsible for reviewing and testing input procedures, monitoring processing, and reviewing and distributing outputs.

Other technical services might include telecommunications, systems programming or technical support, and security administration.

- **Telecommunications** is responsible for maintaining and enhancing computer networks and network connections.
- A **systems programmer** or **technical support** is responsible for updating and maintaining the operating systems.
- **Security administration** is responsible for security of the system including control of access and maintenance of user passwords.

Controls in an IT Environment

As a result of limited segregation of duties and a reduced paper audit trail, the auditor will often have to rely more heavily on the ability to reduce control risk rather than detection risk in order to keep audit risk at an acceptably low level.

The objectives of controls in an IT environment are:

- Completeness
- Accuracy
- Validity
- Authorization
- Timeliness
- Integrity

Controls will include general controls, application controls, input controls, processing controls, and output controls

General Controls

General controls ensure that the control environment is stable and well managed so that application controls are effective. They relate to personnel policies, file security, contingency planning, computer facilities, and access to computer files.

- **Personnel policies** provide for proper separation of duties and the use of computer accounts that provide users with passwords or other means of preventing unauthorized access
- **File security policies** safeguard files from accidental or intentional errors or abuse. Security controls involve internal and external file labels, creating backup copies of critical files, lockout procedures, and file protection

Contingency Planning

Unanticipated interruptions are avoided through **contingency planning** that includes fault tolerant systems and backup files. One approach to backup is the **grandfather-parent-child** procedure in which three generations of files are retained.

A contingency plan will include a **disaster recovery plan** to prepare for the possibility of fires, floods, earthquakes, or terrorist bombings. The plan should specify backup sites to be used for alternate processing.

- A **hot site** is a location that includes a computer system that is already configured similarly to the system regularly used by the company, allowing for immediate use.
- A **cold site** is a location where power and space are available allowing for the installation of processing equipment on short notice.

Controls over **computer facilities** should include locating the facility in a safe place, limiting access to appropriate employees, and maintaining insurance.

Passwords or other forms of identification should be used to limit **access to computer files**.

Application Controls

Application controls include

- **Preventive controls** designed to prevent errors and fraud
- **Detective controls** and **automated controls** are designed to detect errors and fraud
- **User controls** and **corrective controls** allow individual users to follow up on detected errors and fraud

In an IT environment, application controls relate to data input, data processing, and data output.

Input Controls

Input controls are designed to ensure the validity, accuracy, and completeness of data entered into the system. Errors can be avoided through:

- Observational controls
- Use of point of sale devices, such as scanners, to gather and record data automatically

The use of preprinted recording forms can minimize errors.

Data transcription controls, such as preformatted screens, can minimize errors when converting data to machine-readable form.

Edit Tests

Edit tests scrutinize data as it is input to determine if it is in an appropriate form. When not in appropriate form, transactions will be rejected and an exception report will be created. Examples include:

- Tests of numeric field content
- Tests of alphabetic field content
- Tests of alphanumeric field content
- Tests for valid codes
- Tests of reasonableness
- Tests of sign
- Tests of completeness
- Tests of sequence
- Tests of consistency

Other input controls may include an unfound-record test, or a check digit control procedure, or self-checking digit

Processing Controls

Processing controls ensure that data is properly processed. Processing controls ensure that the data is complete and accurate when input. This can be done through a variety of **control totals**.

- As data is prepared for input, a control total is calculated.
- As the computer processes the data, it compares the control total to the actual data processed.
- Any discrepancy between the data processed and the control total would be noted as an exception.

Control totals include **record counts**; **financial control totals**; **nonfinancial control totals**, and **hash totals**.

Once data has been input, processing controls ensure that the data is properly manipulated to produce meaningful output.

- Systems and software documentation allows system analysts to verify that processing programs are complete and thorough
- Computer programs can be tested using error testing compilers to ensure that they do not contain programming language errors
- Test data exposes the program to one sample of each type of exception condition likely to occur during its use
- System testing can be used to make certain that programs within the system are interacting properly

Output Controls

Output controls ensure that the processing results are valid and monitor the distribution and use of output. The completeness, accuracy, and validity of processing results can be checked using activity listings.

The distribution and use of output can be monitored using numbered forms, distribution lists, and requiring signatures for certain reports.

When information is particularly sensitive, users might be instructed to use paper shredders to dispose of reports after use.

The Use of Microcomputers

Microcomputers present additional control risks since they are small and portable, making them easier to steal or damage. Data and software are also more accessible in a microcomputer environment and individuals can more readily access unauthorized records and modify, copy, or destroy data and software.

A variety of controls can be employed in a microcomputer environment

- Maintain an inventory listing of all microcomputer equipment and the purposes for which it is used
- Keyboard locks can be built into the CPUs of microcomputers so that unauthorized users will not have access
- Microcomputers and monitors can be secured to desks or fixtures to discourage theft
- Passwords that are changed periodically limit the access of unauthorized users to sensitive data
- Periodic backup of data on microcomputers enables recovery in the case of alteration or destruction of data
- Sensitive information can be maintained in offline storage kept in locked cabinets to prevent unauthorized access

Auditing Through the Computer

Once the auditor obtains an understanding of internal control, a decision will be made as to the planned assessed level of control risk.

- The auditor may plan to assess control risk at the maximum when the client's computer system is relatively simple and there is a sufficient audit trail.
- When the client's computer system is complex, the lack of an audit trail may prevent the auditor from adequately reducing detection risk through the performance of substantive tests and the auditor will need to set control risk below the maximum. This will require the performance of tests of controls in relation to those control activities on which the auditor intends to rely.

Testing General Control Activities

The auditor will generally first test general control activities. The auditor can test:

- Personnel policies by inspecting personnel manuals, observing the appropriate segregation of duties, and verifying restrictions on the access to the system through the use of passwords
- File security by inspecting external labels on files and using the computer to read internal labels, and observing the existence of lockout procedures and file protection.
- Contingency plans by observing the existence of multiple generations of backup files, discussing disaster recovery plans with management, and observing the existence of a hot or cold site.
- Facilities by observing the appropriateness of the location and the limitations on access and by confirming the existence of insurance.
- Access to computer files by verifying the use of passwords to prevent unauthorized individuals from obtaining access.

Testing Application Control Activities

If general controls are in place and operating effectively, reliance may also be placed on application control activities. The auditor can test input and output controls largely through observation. Processing controls, on the other hand, may be tested in a variety of ways.

In testing controls over the development of, and changes to, programs and systems design, the auditor might:

- Make inquiries of personnel
- Review minutes of meetings of computer staff and users
- Inspect documentation of testing performed before programs were put into use
- Review documentation of program changes and compare them to management approvals
- Inspect manuals being used by operators and other users

Computer assisted audit techniques, or **CAATs**, are used to test the operation of software. These include test data, controlled programs, integrated test facilities, program analysis, tagging and tracing, and generalized audit software programs.

Test data includes one example of each type of exception and is run through the company's computer programs. The auditor compares results to expected results to evaluate the processing of the data and handling of exceptions.

Controlled programs are copies of the client's programs that are under the control of the auditor. The auditor processes the client's data using these programs and compares the results to those of the client to evaluate the client's processing of the data.

Using an **integrated test facility**, fictitious and real transactions are processed simultaneously using the client's system. The auditor can review the client's processing of the data to evaluate the effectiveness of the programs.

Program analysis techniques involve the use of software that will allow the computer to generate flowcharts of other programs. The auditor can examine the flowcharts to evaluate the effectiveness of the client's programs.

By **tagging** transactions, they may be **traced** through the system and the auditor is provided a printout of the steps followed in processing them.

Generalized audit software packages test the reliability of the client's programs. These packages are used to perform many specific audit procedures. One application is **parallel simulation** in which the software is designed to process data in a manner that is essentially the same as that used by the client's program.

Auditing With the Computer

The auditor may use the computer to perform substantive tests. Once the auditor has access to the client's data, the computer can be used to:

- Examine the client's data for validity, completeness, and accuracy
- Rearrange and analyze the client's data
- Select client data for audit samples
- Compare similar data contained in two or more of the client's files to identify discrepancies
- Compare the result of audit procedures, such as test counts, to the client's data

The use of computers in the performance of an audit does not change the auditor's responsibility to adhere to the standards of fieldwork. Methods, however, may change. There may be a reduction in the use of working papers to reduce the auditor's ability to observe the details of calculations when reviewing the work of staff assistants.

Sampling

Sampling is used in both tests of controls & substantive testing

- Nonstatistical samples are based exclusively on auditor's judgment
- Statistical samples involve mathematics & probabilities

Sampling Risk

Audit risk is affected by sampling risk

- Sample for performance of tests may not be representative of population
- Conclusions drawn may not be same as if sample was representative

Sampling Risk & Tests of Control

When sample not representative in a test of control, 2 possible errors:

Risk of Assessing Risk Too High (Underreliance) – Auditor will conclude that control is not effective when it actually is

- Auditor will inappropriately assess level of control risk at maximum & perform more substantive testing than necessary
- Resulting audit will be inefficient

Risk of Assessing Risk Too Low (Overreliance) – Auditor will conclude that control is effective when it actually is not

- Auditor will inappropriately assess level of control risk below the maximum & perform less substantive testing than necessary
- Resulting audit may be ineffective & auditor may issue inappropriate report

Sampling errors in tests of controls

Error rate in sample	Higher than in population	Lower than in population
Resulting error	Underreliance	Overreliance
Effect on audit	Inefficient	Potentially ineffective

Sampling Risk & Substantive Tests

When sample not representative in a substantive test, 2 possible errors:

Risk of Incorrect Rejection – Auditor will incorrectly conclude that management assertion is not corroborated

- Auditor will reject sample
- Auditor will require inappropriate adjustment or issue inappropriately modified report

Risk of Incorrect Acceptance – Auditor will incorrectly conclude that management assertion is corroborated

- Auditor will accept sample
- Auditor will inappropriately issue unmodified report

Sampling errors in substantive tests

Error rate in sample	Higher than in population	Lower than in population
Resulting error	Incorrect rejection	Incorrect acceptance
Effect on audit	Incorrect modified report	Incorrect unmodified report

Types of Statistical Sampling

There are 3 types of statistical sampling frequently used in auditing

Attribute sampling – generally used for tests of controls

- Estimate frequency of errors in population based on frequency in sample
- Determine whether or not estimated error rate indicates control is working effectively

Variables sampling – generally used for substantive testing

- Estimate value of population based on value of items in sample
- Determine whether or not estimated value is close enough management's assertion as to valuation

Probability proportional to size sampling – also used for substantive testing

- Form of variables sampling
- Items that are larger in size or value higher probability of being selected for sample

Attribute Sampling

The auditor determines the control to be tested & identifies the type of error that would indicate the control is not effective so that a sampling plan can be established

1) Establish **tolerable deviation rate** – the maximum error rate the auditor will allow without increasing the assessed level of control risk

2) Determine **allowable risk of overreliance** or sampling risk – the maximum allowable risk of assessing control risk too low

3) Determine the **expected population deviation rate** – the rate of errors expected to occur in population which is the basis for the initial assessed level of control risk

4) Calculate the **sample size**

5) Select & test the sample

Attribute Sampling (continued)

6) Calculate the sample deviation rate - # of errors in sample ÷ # of items in sample

7) Calculate **upper deviation limit** – maximum population error rate based on sample deviation rate & acceptable risk of overreliance

   Upper precision limit = sample deviation rate + allowance for sampling risk

8) Reach conclusions & document results

   - If upper precision limit ≤ tolerable rate – assessed level of control risk unchanged
   - If upper precision limit > tolerable rate – assessed level of control risk increased

Calculating Sample Size

Various factors affect sample size

Factor	*Relationship to sample size*	*Effect*
Tolerable rate	Inverse	The lower the tolerable rate, the larger the sample
Allowable risk of assessing control risk too low	Inverse	The higher the allowable risk of overreliance, the smaller the sample
Expected population deviation rate	Direct	The higher the expected population deviation rate, the larger the sample
Population size		Population size has very slight effect on sample size unless population is very small

Variations of Attribute Sampling

Different approaches can be used when applying attribute sampling

Under traditional attribute sampling, sample size is determined & sample tested to estimate error rate in population

Under **stop or go (sequential) sampling,** testing discontinues when auditor acquires sufficient data

- Appropriate when expected deviation rate is low
- Sample selected in steps
- Each step is based on results of previous step
- No fixed sample size and may result in lower sample if few or no errors detected

Under **discovery sampling**, sample size is very small

- Appropriate when expected deviation rate is extremely low or zero
- Sample large enough to detect at least 1 error if it exists
- Any errors in sample results in rejection

Variables Sampling

The auditor determines the balance to be tested & a sampling plan can be established

1) Establish **tolerable misstatement** – the maximum difference, taking materiality into account, between the actual balance & the reported balance that will not prevent the auditor from issuing an unmodified report
2) Determine **allowable risk of incorrect acceptance** or sampling risk – the maximum allowable risk of that the auditor will accept an amount that is materially incorrect
3) Determine the **expected amount of misstatement** or expected deviation – the amount by which the auditor expects the actual balance to differ from the reported amount based on the **assessed level of control risk**
4) Calculate the **sample size**
5) Select & test the sample

Variables Sampling (continued)

6) Calculate the **upper deviation limit** – the estimated difference between the actual amount & the reported amount based on the sample

7) Reach conclusions & document results

   - If precision ≤ tolerable misstatement – opinion may require modification
   - If precision > tolerable misstatement – opinion will not require modification

Allowable risk of Incorrect Acceptance

The allowable risk of incorrect acceptance can be calculated based on other factors

1) Determine acceptable audit risk (AR)
2) Measure inherent risk (IR)
3) Assess level of control risk (CR)
4) Use AR, IR, & CR to calculate acceptable level of detection risk (DR)

   AR ÷ (IR X CR) = DR

5) At various levels of DR, measure the allowable risk of incorrect acceptance

   Allowable level of incorrect acceptance = AR ÷ (IR X CR X DR)

Example:

If AR = 5%, IR = 100%, & CR is assessed at 50%

DR = .05 ÷ (1.00 X .50) = .10 or 10%

If DR is set at 30%

Allowable level of incorrect acceptance = .05 ÷ (1.00 X .50 X .30) = .333 or 33 1/3%

Calculating Sample Size

Various factors affect sample size

Factor	*Relationship to sample size*	*Effect*
Tolerable misstatement	Inverse	The lower the tolerable misstatement, the larger the sample
Allowable risk of incorrect acceptance	Inverse	The higher the allowable risk of incorrect acceptance, the lower the expected reliability, and the smaller the sample
Expected amount of misstatement	Direct	The higher the expected amount of misstatement, the larger the sample
Assessed level of control risk	Direct	The higher the assessed level of control risk, the larger the sample
Population size	Direct	The larger the population, the larger the sample size

Probability Proportional to Size (PPS) Sampling

PPS, a form of dollar unit sampling, has advantages over classical variables sampling

- Items with larger dollar amounts have a greater probability of being selected
- An item that is individually material will automatically be selected
- Sample size may be reduced as the same item may be selected more than once
- The sample distribution does not have to be close to the distribution in the population for the sample to be valid
- Sampling can be initiated prior to year end more easily

Disadvantages of PPS

- Understated items have a lower probability of being selected
- Items with zero or negative balances are not generally included in the sample
- A high frequency of misstatements results in an increase in sample size

PPS is most effective when:

- Few or no errors are expected
- The auditor is concerned about overstatement of the account

PPS (continued)

PPS is applied as follows

1) Determine the risk of incorrect acceptance & the estimated number of overstatement errors
2) Measure the necessary reliability factor for errors of overstatement
    - Measured by formula (selected from table)
    - The higher the risk of incorrect acceptance, the lower the reliability
    - The higher the estimated number of overstatement errors, the higher the reliability
3) Determine the tolerable misstatement
4) Determine sampling interval

    Sampling interval = tolerable misstatement ÷ reliability factor

5) Calculate sample size

    Sample size = total dollar amount of population ÷ sampling interval

6) Select & test sample
7) Calculate projected error in population
8) Evaluate sample results & draw conclusion

Selecting the Sample

1) List items in population in logical sequence

2) Based on the amount of an item and the total amounts of all previous items, each item will represent a cumulative amount

3) Assign each item a range of values
   - The lower end of the range will be the previous item's cumulative amount
   - The upper end of the range will be the item's cumulative amount

4) Select the items within the population where a multiple of the sampling interval is included in the range

Calculating the Projected Error

1) Determine items in sample containing misstatement

2) If item has dollar amount ≥ sampling interval, misstatement is added to projected error

3) If item has dollar amount < sampling interval, effect of misstatement on projected error must be calculated & added to the projected error

    - Calculate a tainting factor = amount of misstatement ÷ dollar amount of item
    - Projected error = tainting factor X sampling interval

Application of PPS Sampling

1) Assume the following

- Sales consists of 250 sales transactions totaling $100,000
- The auditor expects only 2 errors
- The tolerable misstatement is $6,000
- The risk of incorrect acceptance is 10%

The first 10 invoices are in the following amounts

Inv #	*Amt*	*Cum amt*	*Range*	*Inv #*	*Amt*	*Cum amt*	*Range*
#1	$600	$600	$0-$600	**#6**	$2,170	$4,750	2,581-4,750
#2	355	955	601-955	**#7**	35	4,785	4,751-4,785
#3	170	1,125	956-1,125	**#8**	20	4,805	4,786-4,805
#4	860	1,985	1,126-1,985	**#9**	1,625	6,430	4,806-6,430
#5	595	2,580	1,986-2,580	**#10**	15	6,445	6,431-6,445

2) Reliability factor will be selected from the following table

Risk of incorrect acceptance	*1%*	*5%*	***10%***	*15%*
Estimated # of errors				
0	4.61	3.00	2.31	1.90
1	6.64	4.75	3.89	3.38
2	8.41	6.30	**5.33**	4.72

Reliability factor will be 5.33

3) Sampling interval = $6,000 ÷ 5.33 = $1,126

4) Sample size = $100,000 ÷ $1,126 = 89 items

5) Selecting sample

Inv #4 includes $1,126
Inv #5 includes $2,252
Inv #6 includes 3,378
Inv #6 includes 4,504
Inv #9 includes 5,630

} Sample consists of invoices 4, 5, 6, & 9

6) Compare audited amount to recorded amount & project error

Inv #	*Recorded amount*	*Audited amount*	*Over-statement*	*Tainting Factor*	*Sampling Interval*	*Projected Error*
#4	$860	$840	$20	2.3%	$1,226	$28
#5	595	575	20	3.4%	1,226	42
#6	2,170	2,100	70	n/a	n/a	70
#9	1,625	1,585	40	n/a	n/a	40
Projected error based on first 10 invoices						$180

7) When sample is completed, if projected error ≤ $6,000, auditor will conclude that sales is not materially misstated

Audit Reports

Auditor must adhere to 4 standards of reporting

1) Indicate conformity with **GA**AP
2) Identify **in**consistencies from prior period
3) Indicate if not **a**dequate **d**isclosure
4) Express **o**pinion or indicate why not & indicate degree of **re**sponsibility taken

*With a good report, you **GAin** respect and others will **adore** you*

Standard Report - An Unqualified Opinion

When the auditor has gathered sufficient competent evidential matter to corroborate management's assertions, an unqualified opinion is expressed in a standard report

- The title of the report will indicate that the auditor is independent
- The report is addressed to the whoever hired the auditor, may be directors, the shareholders, a third party requesting the audit, or, in public companies, the audit committee
- An introductory paragraph will discuss the nature of the engagement
- A scope paragraph will describe the work performed
- An opinion paragraph will provide appropriate assurances
- The report is signed by the auditor
- The report is dated as of the completion of field work

Introductory Paragraph

The introductory paragraph describes the nature of the engagement

- Identifies financial statements audited
- Indicates management's responsibility for the financial statements
- Indicates auditor's responsibility to express an opinion

"We have audited the accompanying balance sheet of X Company as of December 31, 19XX, and the related statements of income, retained earnings, and cash flows for the year then ended. These financial statements are the responsibility of the Company's management. Our responsibility is to express an opinion on these financial statements based on our audit."

Scope Paragraph

The scope paragraph describes the work performed

- Audit conducted in accordance with GAAS
- Obtained reasonable assurance about material misstatements
- Examined evidence to support financial statements
- Assessed accounting principles & estimates used by management
- Evaluated overall financial statement presentation
- Believed audit is reasonable basis for opinion

"We conducted our audit in accordance with generally accepted auditing standards. Those standards require that we plan and perform the audit to obtain reasonable assurance about whether the financial statements are free of material misstatement. An audit includes examining, on a test basis, evidence supporting the amounts and disclosures in the financial statements. An audit also includes assessing the accounting principles used and significant estimates made by management, as well as evaluating the overall financial statement presentation. We believe that our audit provides a reasonable basis for our opinion."

Opinion Paragraph

The opinion paragraph provides those assurances that can be supported by the audit

- Expresses opinion on the fair presentation of the financial statements
- Indicates limitation of materiality
- Indicates conformity with GAAP

"In our opinion, the financial statements referred to above present fairly, in all material respects, the financial position of X Company as of December 31, 19XX, and the results of operations and its cash flows for the year then ended in conformity with GAAP."

The opinion paragraph addresses the requirements of the standards of reporting

1) Explicitly indicates conformity with GAAP
2) Implicitly indicates consistency by not identifying inconsistencies
3) Implicitly indicates adequacy of disclosure by not stating otherwise
4) Explicitly expresses an opinion on the financial statements
5) Implicitly indicates auditor is taking full responsibility unless modified to explicitly indicate division of responsibility

Modified Reports

Various issues arising during the course of an audit may cause the auditor to modify the report

Different modifications have different levels of significance

1) May have no effect on assurances given by auditor
   - Emphasis of a matter
   - Division of responsibility
2) May reduce assurances – qualified opinion
3) May negate assurances
   - Disclaimer of opinion
   - Adverse opinion

Emphasis of a Matter

1) Auditor has corroborated management's assertions regarding the matter

    - **R** & O - The company has the rights or obligations indicated by the related items on the financial statements
    - **A** or V – The auditor accepts the amount at which the item is reported
    - **C** – All transactions, events, or circumstances that relate to the item occurring during the current period have been taken into account
    - **E** or O – The item does exist or the transaction did occur
    - **D** & P – The item is adequately disclosed & is presented on the financial statements in conformity with GAAP

4) Auditor expresses unqualified opinion with standard introductory, scope, & opinion paragraphs

5) Auditor believes users will better understand information in financial statements or report with additional information

6) Auditor adds explanatory paragraph, after opinion paragraph to emphasize the matter

Emphasis of a Matter (continued)

Items that might be emphasized in an explanatory paragraph may include:

- Justifiable departure from GAAP
- Justifiable lack of consistency
- Division of responsibility with another auditor
- Change in opinion regarding prior period's statements on comparative financial statements
- Omission of supplementary information required by the FASB or the GASB or quarterly financial information required by the SEC
- Material inconsistency between unaudited information in the document with the financial statements & information in the financial statements
- Unusual or significant transaction requiring emphasis
- Emphasis of an uncertainty (at auditor's discretion)
- Uncertainty raising going concern doubts

Emphasis of an Uncertainty (at Auditor's Discretion)

1) Auditor has corroborated management assertions regarding the uncertainty
    - Management has assessed likelihood of loss
    - Management has reasonably estimated the amount of loss, if possible
    - Management has properly accrued or disclosed the uncertainty

Likelihood of loss	*Amount of loss estimable*	*Amount of loss not estimable*
Probable	Accrue & disclose	Disclose only
Reasonably possible	Disclose only	Disclose only
Remote	Neither accrue nor disclose	Neither accrue nor disclose

1) Auditor expresses unqualified opinion
2) Auditor modifies report by adding paragraph emphasizing uncertainty after opinion paragraph
3) Management may not properly accrue or disclose uncertainty
    - Represents departure from GAAP
    - Requires modification of opinion

Uncertainty Raising Going Concern Doubts

Auditor may conclude there is substantial doubt of entity's ability to continue as going concern for reasonable period

- Reasonable period assumed to be up to one year beyond date of financial statements
- Auditor may still express an unqualified opinion
- Auditor modifies report by adding explanatory paragraph after opinion paragraph

Conditions & events may raise going concern to doubts

- Operating losses, negative cash flows, or other negative trends
- Loan defaults, dividend arrearages, or other indications of financial difficulty
- Labor difficulties or other internal matters
- Obsolescence of patents, declining industry, or other external matters

Management's plans may reduce doubts

- Disposal of assets
- Reduction of discretionary expenditures
- Increase in equity or decrease in dividend requirements

Uncertainty Raising Going Concern Doubts (continued)

Audit procedures may identify going concern issues

- Analytical procedures
- Review of subsequent events
- Examination of debt agreements to determine compliance
- Reading of minutes of board meetings
- Making inquiry of legal counsel
- Confirming with others arrangements for financial support

Division of Responsibility

Fourth standard of reporting requires clear-cut indication of degree of responsibility taken

The work may be performed entirely by the auditor & assistants

- Report is not modified
- Report implies that auditor is taking full responsibility

Work may be performed by other auditor

- Auditor must determine if work of other auditor is reliable
- Auditor may take responsibility for work of other auditor
- Auditor may indicate division of responsibility for work performed by other auditor

If work of other auditor is not reliable

- Constitutes scope limitation
- Auditor will modify opinion

Auditor Takes Responsibility

Before taking responsibility for work of other auditor

- Auditor should be satisfied of other auditor's independence & professional reputation
- Auditor should consider performing additional procedures

Procedures may include:

- Visiting the other auditor
- Discussing audit procedures & conclusion
- Review the other auditor's audit programs
- Review the other auditor's working papers

If auditor decides to take responsibility

- Unqualified opinion expressed
- Unmodified report issued with no reference to other auditor

Auditor Does Not Take Responsibility

A division of responsibility must be clearly indicated in report

- Introductory paragraph indicates portion of work performed by other auditor in percentages or dollars
- Scope paragraph indicates work of other auditor as part of basis of opinion
- Opinion paragraph refers to work of other auditor as part of basis for opinion

Modifications to the report:

- Will be specific as to the portions of the work was performed by the other auditor
- Will not generally name other auditor
- Other auditor may be named if permission is received & their report is included in the document containing the financial statements

Scope Limitations

Scope limitations are restrictions on the actions of the auditor

- Prevent auditor from performing procedures as planned
- May be imposed by client
- May result from circumstances

Types of Scope Limitations

Examples of scope limitations include:

- Auditor unable to confirm accounts receivable by direct communication
- Auditor unable to obtain audited financial statements of investee
- Auditor unable to observe ending inventory
- Auditor unable to obtain letter from attorney
- Client's accounting records inadequate
- Client does not provide all documents, such as minutes of director meetings
- Client will not sign management representation letter

Overcoming Scope Limitations

Auditor may be able to overcome scope limitations

- Assertion that cannot be corroborated may not be material to financial statements taken as a whole
- Auditor may be able to apply alternate procedures

When auditor can overcome scope limitation

- Unqualified opinion expressed
- Unmodified report issued

Modified Reports

When auditor cannot overcome scope limitation

- Effect of scope limitation is evaluated
- Modified report issued

Scope limitation may be material

- Auditor able to express opinion on financial statements taken as a whole
- Material assertion neither corroborated nor contradicted
- Auditor issues qualified opinion

Scope limitation may be pervasive (very material)

- Auditor unable to express opinion on financial statements taken as a whole
- Auditor issues disclaimer of opinion

Qualified Opinion Due to Scope Limitation

Affects auditor's report in 3 respects:

1) Scope paragraph modified to alert user to limitation

   "*Except as discussed in the following paragraph*, we conducted our audit…"

2) Explanatory paragraph added after scope paragraph to describe limitation

3) Opinion paragraph refers to scope limitation to limit assurance provided by opinion

   "In our opinion, *except for the possible effects of…*, the financial statements referred to above…"

Scope Limitation Related to Beginning Inventory

A special scope limitation occurs when the auditor is unable to obtain sufficient competent evidential matter to corroborate management's assertion as to the value of beginning inventory

Affects auditor's report in 4 respects:

1) Standard introductory paragraph

2) Scope paragraph modified to alert user to limitation

   "*Except as discussed in the following paragraph*, we conducted our audit…"

3) Explanatory paragraph added after scope paragraph to describe limitation in regard to beginning inventory

4) A paragraph is added before the opinion paragraph disclaiming an opinion on the statements of income, retained earnings, & cash flows

5) Opinion paragraph modified to express opinion on balance sheet only

Departures From GAAP

Examples of departures from GAAP include:

- Principles selected & applied not generally accepted
- Principles selected are not appropriate under the circumstances
- Information in the financial statements is not classified & summarized in reasonable manner
- Financial statements do not fairly present financial position, results of operations, and cash flows within a range of acceptable limits

Materiality

The materiality of a departure from GAAP will determine its effect on the auditor's report

- If not material, unmodified report issued
- If material, qualified opinion expressed
- If pervasive (very material), adverse opinion expressed

Qualified Opinion Due to Departure From GAAP

Affects auditor's report in 2 respects:

1) Standard introductory & scope paragraphs

2) Explanatory paragraph added after scope paragraph to describe departure

3) Opinion paragraph refers to departure from GAAP, limiting assurance provided by opinion

   "In our opinion, *except for the effects of...*, the financial statements referred to above..."

Adverse Opinion Due to Departure From GAAP

An adverse opinion indicates that the financial statements are not fairly presented

Affects auditor's report in 2 respects:

1) Standard introductory & scope paragraphs
2) Explanatory paragraph added after scope paragraph to describe departure
3) Opinion paragraph refers to departure from GAAP & negates assurance provided by opinion

   "In our opinion, *because of the effects of the matters discussed in the preceding paragraph,* the financial statements referred to above *do not* present fairly..."

Inconsistencies

Most changes in accounting principles affect consistency:

- A change from one acceptable principle to another
- A change from an unacceptable principle to an acceptable one
- A change in principle that is inseparable from a change in estimate
- A change in the method of accounting for subsidiaries
- A change in the companies included in consolidated financial statements

Certain changes do not affect consistency

- A change in accounting estimate
- A correction of an error
- A change in classification
- Adoption of a principle for a new transaction
- Changes that will affect future financial statements but not those of prior periods

Effect of Inconsistency

Auditor may determine that inconsistency is justified

- Unqualified opinion expressed
- Report modified by adding paragraph after the opinion paragraph to emphasize the inconsistency

Auditor may determine that inconsistency is not justified

- Qualified opinion expressed
- Report modified

Qualified Opinion Due to Inconsistency

Affects auditor's report in 2 respects:

1) Standard introductory & scope paragraphs
2) Explanatory paragraph added after scope paragraph to describe change
3) Opinion paragraph refers to change in accounting principle, limiting assurance provided by opinion

   "In our opinion, *except for the change in accounting principle discussed in the preceding paragraph*, the financial statements referred to above..."

Inadequate Disclosure

The audit report implies that disclosure is adequate by not mentioning disclosure

Effect of omitted disclosure depends on materiality

- If material, auditor issues qualified opinion
- If very material, auditor issues adverse opinion

Qualified Opinion Due to Inadequate Disclosure

Affects auditor's report in 2 respects:

1) Standard introductory & scope paragraphs
2) Explanatory paragraph added after scope paragraph to describe nature of omitted disclosure
3) Opinion paragraph refers to omitted disclosure, limiting assurance provided by opinion

   "In our opinion, *except for the omission of the information discussed in the preceding paragraph*, the financial statements referred to above…"

When statement of cash flows is omitted:

1) Introductory paragraph modified to omit reference to statement of cash flows
2) Standard scope paragraphs
3) Explanatory paragraph added after scope paragraph to indicate omission of statement of cash flows
4) Opinion paragraph refers to omitted statement of cash flows

   "In our opinion, *except that the omission of a statement of cash flows results in an incomplete presentation as explained in the preceding paragraph*, the financial statements referred to above…"

Comparative Financial Statements

When financial statements for 2 or more periods are presented in comparative form, the auditor's report applies to all of the financial statements presented

A continuing auditor may issue a standard report with an unqualified opinion

- Only appropriate when unqualified opinion had been issued on prior periods' financial statements
- Language in introductory & scope paragraphs modified to refer to audits, rather than audit
- Language in introductory & opinion paragraph modified to refer to all financial statements presented
- Report dated as of completion of field work of most recent period

Differing Opinions

The auditor may have expressed an opinion on a prior period's financial statements that is different from the opinion on the current period's statements

1) The introductory & scope paragraphs will be the same as if unqualified opinions had been issued

2) The explanatory paragraph after the scope paragraph will indicate specifically to which period or periods the exception applies

3) The opinion paragraph will also indicate specifically to which period or periods the exception applies

Scope Limitation Related to Beginning Inventory

The auditor may not be able to obtain sufficient competent evidential matter to corroborate management's assertion as to the value of beginning inventory for the earliest period presented

Affects auditor's report in 4 respects:

1) The introductory paragraph will be the same as if unqualified opinions had been issued
2) Scope paragraph modified to alert user to limitation

   "*Except as explained in the following paragraph*, we conducted our audit…"
3) Explanatory paragraph added after scope paragraph to describe limitation in regard to beginning inventory of earliest period
4) A paragraph is added before the opinion paragraph disclaiming an opinion on the statements of income, retained earnings, & cash flows for the earliest period presented
5) Opinion paragraph modified to express opinion on balance sheet only for earliest period presented, but all financial statements of remaining periods

Updating a Prior Period's Opinion

Reasons for a modified opinion issued in a prior period may have been corrected, resulting in an unqualified opinion for all periods presented

Affects auditor's report in 1 respect:

1) The introductory, scope, & opinion paragraphs will be the same as if unqualified opinions had been issued for all periods presented
2) Explanatory paragraph added after scope paragraph to describe reasons for change in opinion related to prior period

When an uncertainty from a prior period has been resolved

1) The same report is issued as if unqualified opinions had been issued for all periods presented
2) Any reference to the uncertainty in a prior period's report would be omitted

Audited & Unaudited Financial Statements

Unaudited financial statements presented in comparative form with audited financial statements must be clearly marked as unaudited

In addition, either:

- The report on the prior period's financial statements may be reissued along with the report on the current period's financial statements
- The report on the current period's financial statements may include a paragraph describing the degree of responsibility being assumed for the prior period's financial statements

Noncontinuing Auditor

The auditor of the current period's financial statements may not have been the auditor for the financial statements of prior periods being presented in comparative form

- The predecessor may agree to reissue the report previously issued
- The predecessor may decide not to reissue the report

Reissuance of Predecessor's Report

If the predecessor's report is to be reissued, the predecessor should

- Consider whether report is still appropriate
- Compare the prior period's financial statements to those being presented
- Obtain an updated management letter of representations

The predecessor may become aware of information that affects the financial statements or the opinion expressed

- If no restatement or revision is necessary, the predecessor's report will have its original date
- If the financial statements are restated or revised, the predecessor's report should be dual dated

Predecessor's Report Not Reissued

Current period's auditor should not name the predecessor auditor in the report

The introductory paragraph of the report will be modified:

1) Indicate that prior periods' financial statements were audited by another auditor
2) Provide the date of the predecessor's report
3) Indicate the type of report that had been issued
4) Give substantive reasons for modifications to the report on the prior periods

Restrictions on an Auditor's Report

Certain circumstances will make it appropriate to restrict distribution or use of an auditor's report.

- When financial statements are prepared according to provisions of **contractual agreements**, the report should be restricted to parties to the contract
- When financial statements are prepared according to **regulations**, the report should be restricted to the regulatory agency
- When the report indicates the findings of **agreed-upon procedures**, the report should be restricted to the parties agreeing upon the procedures

The client should be informed of the restriction

The report should include a final paragraph stating the restriction

By-Product Reports

Reports may be issued as a by-product of an audit. These may include:

- Reports on internal control
- Communication with the audit committee
- Reports on compliance with contractual provisions or regulations

These reports should be restricted to the audit committee, management, specified regulatory agencies, or parties to the contract.

The report should state:

- Procedures performed were designed to enable the expression of an opinion on the financial statements
- Only limited assurance can be provided relative to the specific subject of the report

Compilations & Reviews

Accountants engaged to perform compilations or reviews of nonpublic companies must comply with Statements on Standards for Accounting and Review Services (SSARS)

Compilations

Accountants provide no assurance regarding financial statements in a compilation

- Accountant presents information in the form of financial statements
- Information is representation of management

Accountant does not gather evidence in relation to financial statements

- Should read compiled financial statements
- Determine if financial statements appear to be in appropriate form & free from obvious error

Compilation Report

Report on compilation of financial statements of nonpublic company should state:

- Compilation performed in accordance with SSARS issued by the AICPA
- Compilation limited to presenting management's information in the form of financial statements
- Financial statements not audited or reviewed
- Accountant does not express opinion or provide any other form of assurance

In addition:

- Report dated as of completion of compilation
- Each page of compiled financial statements should refer to report

"See Accountant's Compilation Report"

An accountant need not be independent to perform a compilation

When not independent, last paragraph of report should so indicate

"We are not independent with respect to X Company"

Omission of Disclosures

Accountant may compile financial statements of nonpublic company when substantially all disclosures omitted

- Omission must be indicated in report
- Omission not intended to make financial statements misleading

Reviews

Accountants provide limited assurance regarding financial statements in a review

- Accountant must be independent to perform review
- Accountant performs inquiries & analytical procedures (APs)

Examples of inquiries & APs performed in a review include:

- Inquire about accounting principles
- Inquire about procedures for recording, classifying, & summarizing information for financial statements
- Identify unusual relationship & unusual items using APs
- Inquire about actions taken at meeting of shareholders, directors, or others that may affect financial statements
- Read financial statements to determine if they appear to conform with GAAP
- Obtain reports from other accountants auditing or reviewing components of the financial statements
- Inquire of individuals responsible for financial & accounting matters

Accountant does not obtain understanding of internal control or assess control risk

Accountant must obtain a representation letter from management

Review Report

Report on reviewed financial statements should state:

- A review was performed in accordance with SSARS issued by the AICPA
- Information in financial statements is representation of management
- Review consists of inquiries & APs
- Review is substantially less than audit intended to express opinion on financial statements
- No opinion is expressed
- Accountant not aware of material modifications needed to conform financial statements to GAAP unless indicated in report

Report dated as of completion of inquiries & APs

Each page of reviewed financial statements should refer to report

"See Accountant's Review Report"

Accountant may also perform a review on only one financial statement provided scope of inquiries & APs not limited

Departures From GAAP

Accountant may become aware of material departure from GAAP

- Should request that financial statements be revised
- If not revised, should consider modification of report
- If modification not adequate, accountant should consider withdrawing from engagement

Downgrading Engagements

Accountant may be asked to downgrade an engagement that has begun

- Audit may be downgraded to review or compilation
- Review may be downgraded to compilation

Before accepting downgrade, accountant should consider:

- Reason given by client
- Additional effort to complete original engagement
- Additional cost to complete original engagement

Additional Audit Issues

Subsequent Events

Subsequent events occur after the balance sheet date but before issuance of the financial statements

Subsequent event may relate to condition existing at balance sheet date

- Examples may include settlement of litigation or learning of the bankruptcy of a customer
- Effects of these events require adjustment to financial statements

Subsequent event may relate to condition not existing at balance sheet date

- Examples may include sale of securities or loss due to natural disaster
- Effects of these events do not require adjustments to financial statements
- May require disclosure

Subsequent Events (continued)

Procedures after the balance sheet date may include:

- Comparing subsequent interim financial information to audited financial statements
- Making inquiries of management
- Investigating changes in long-term debt
- Reading minutes of board meetings & stockholder meetings
- Making inquiries of legal counsel concerning litigation, claims, & assessments arising after year end

Subsequent Discovery of Facts

After issuing report auditor may become aware of information that existed at balance sheet date

If facts would have affected report:

- Auditor should determine if information is reliable
- Auditor should determine if users are still likely to be relying on report

Auditor should try to prevent further reliance on report

- Advise client to make appropriate disclosure to parties known to be relying on the report
- Client may issued revised financial statements
- Disclosure may be made in imminent subsequent financial statements

In case of refusal by client, notify board of directors of need to take appropriate steps

- May notify client that report should not be associated with financial statements
- May notify regulatory agencies that report should not be relied upon
- May notify each person known to be relying on report that it should not be relied on

Omitted Procedures

Auditor may determine that a substantive procedure considered necessary was not performed during the audit

- Other procedures may have compensated for omission
- Omitted procedure may impair ability to support opinion

Omitted procedure should then be applied

- Alternative procedures may be substituted
- If auditor becomes aware of previously unknown facts, rules for subsequent discovery of facts are applied

Condensed Financial Statements & Selected Data

Auditor may report on condensed financial statements or selected financial data if derived from audited financial statements

Report should indicate

- That the complete financial statements were audited & an opinion was expressed
- The date of the auditor's report on the complete financial statements
- The type of opinion expressed
- Whether the information is fairly stated in all material respects in relation to the complete financial statements

Other Information

Other information may be included in documents containing audited financial statements

The auditor may be responsible for reporting on the information depending on its nature & its relationship to the financial statements

Other information may include:

- Narratives & other information included in documents such as annual reports
- Supplementary information required by the FASB or GASB
- Information accompanying the financial statements in auditor submitted documents
- Segment information

Narratives & Other Information

Auditor's responsibility limited to financial information identified in the report

- No obligation to perform procedures or corroborate information
- Should read information to determine consistency with audited financial statements

In case of inconsistency

- Financial statements or auditor's report may require revision
- Otherwise, client should be asked to revise or eliminate the information

If client refuses, auditor may:

- Revise audit report including separate explanatory paragraph describing the inconsistency
- Withhold use of the report
- Withdraw from the engagement

Supplementary Information Required by the FASB or GASB

When required information supplementary to, but not part of audited financial statements

- Auditor responsible for applying limited procedures
- Auditor responsible for reporting on deficiencies or omissions

Information Accompanying Financial Statements in Document Submitted by Auditor

Auditor may submit document to client or others containing audited financial statements & additional information

- Auditor report covers balance sheet & statements of income, retained earnings, & cash flows
- Additional information may include statistical data, consolidating information, or historical summaries

Auditor must report on all information included in document submitted by auditor

- Audit procedures may be modified to provide basis for opinion on accompanying information
- Measure of materiality same as used in relation to financial statements taken as a whole
- If subjected to audit procedures, auditor may include opinion that accompanying information is fairly stated in the audit report
- If not subjected to audit procedures, auditor may disclaim an opinion and must mark the financial statements as unaudited

Segment Information

When disclosure of segment information is required, may affect auditor's report

- Auditor must evaluate for errors or omissions
- Scope limitation, errors, or omissions will result in qualified opinion
- Segment information not mentioned in report unless there is an exception

Summary of Effects of Other Information

Type of information	*Auditor's responsibility*	*Reporting responsibility*	*Effect on audit report*
Other information	Read for consistency	Report on exceptions only	No effect unless exceptions Explanatory paragraph
Information required by FASB or GASB	Limited review procedures	Report on exceptions only	No effect unless omissions or departures Explanatory paragraph
Information in auditor submitted document	Depends on nature of information	Must report but may disclaim opinion	No effect other than paragraph to discuss information
Segment information	Audit procedures	Report on exceptions only	Qualified opinion if omissions or departures or scope limitation

Letters to Underwriters

Accountants provide letters to underwriters (comfort letters) in connection with the registration of securities with the SEC

- Dated same date or just before registration statement becomes effective
- Accountant's involvement limited to negative assurance
- Not required under Securities Act of 1933 & copies not filed with SEC

Subjects covered in a comfort letter may include:

- Independence of accountants
- Whether audited financial statements & schedules comply in all material respects with requirements of Securities Act of 1933
- Unaudited financial statements, condensed interim information, pro forma financial statements, financial forecasts, & changes in items prepared or occurring after the date of the latest financial statements included in the registration statement
- Tables, statistics, & other information included in the registration statement
- Negative assurance as to compliance of nonfinancial information in registration statement to requirements of Regulation S-K

Statements Used in Other Countries

Auditor may report on financial statements of U.S. entity

- Prepared in conformity with accounting principles of another country
- For use outside of U.S.

Auditor should comply with general standards & standards of field work & must understand accounting principles of other country

If financial statements used exclusively outside U.S., report may be

- Similar to report issued according to GAAS, modified to report on accounting principles of other country
- Report form of the other country

Quality Control

CPA firms should establish quality controls to ensure compliance with professional standards

Nature & extent of quality control policies & procedures will depend on

- Size of firm & number of offices
- Knowledge & experience of personnel & authority allowed to personnel
- Nature & complexity of firm's practice
- Cost-benefit considerations

Policies & procedures should relate to

- Hiring, assigning, & advancement of personnel & professional development
- Accepting & continuing only client's with reasonable assurance of avoiding those whose management lacks integrity
- Maintaining independence, integrity, & objectivity in carrying out professional responsibilities
- Planning, supervising, documenting, & otherwise performing engagements with reasonable assurance of meeting professional standards & regulatory requirements
- Monitoring activities to evaluate effectiveness of quality control policies & procedures

Other Engagements & Reports

Special Reports

An auditor may be called upon to prepare a special report

- Reports are based on some service other than a financial statement audit under GAAS
- Auditor requested to provide some degree of assurance

Types of special reports include reports on

- Financial statements prepared under a comprehensive basis of accounting other than GAAP (OCBOA)
- Specified elements, accounts, or items of a financial statement
- Compliance with aspects of contractual agreements or regulatory requirements
- Financial information provided in prescribed forms or schedules

Financial Statements Prepared in Conformity With an OCBOA

An auditor may report on financial statements of a nonpublic company prepared on the basis of

- Accounting used for tax purposes
- Cash receipts & disbursements
- Accounting required to comply with a regulatory agency
- Another set of criteria having substantial support

The auditor may perform an audit in accordance with GAAS on financial statements prepared in conformity with an OCBOA

The report would be modified as follows

- The identification of the financial statements in the introductory paragraph will refer to titles appropriate for the OCBOA
- An explanatory paragraph will state the basis of accounting used, refer to a footnote describing the OCBOA, & indicate that the basis of accounting is not GAAP
- The opinion paragraph will identify the financial statements & refer to the footnote

Specified Elements, Accounts, or Items of a Financial Statement

An auditor may be requested to express an opinion on one or more specified elements, accounts, or items that are part of a full set of financial statements

- Procedures will be limited to the elements, accounts, or items
- An opinion can be expressed on the elements, accounts, or items subjected to audit procedures

An auditor may also be asked to apply specific agreed upon procedures to elements, accounts, or items that are part of financial statements

- The accountant will perform those specific procedures requested
- The report should summarize the procedures performed & findings
- Distribution of the report will be limited to those establishing the scope of the engagement

Compliance With Aspects of Contractual Agreements or Regulatory Requirements

An entity may be required to provide information indicating compliance with aspects of contractual agreements or regulatory requirements

- The auditor may give negative assurance regarding compliance provided the auditor has audited the financial statements to which the information relates
- The assurance is given in a separate report or in a separate paragraph of the auditor's report

An auditor may also be asked to report on financial presentations prepared to comply with contractual agreements or regulatory requirements

- The financial presentations are generally intended for the use of the contracting parties, the regulatory body, or specified parties
- Use of the report should be limited to those parties

Financial Information in Prescribed Forms or Schedules

Auditors may be asked to complete printed forms or schedules with prescribed wording for the auditor's report

- The auditor must evaluate whether the prescribed forms or schedules conform to applicable professional standards of reporting
- When they do not, the auditor should reword the form or attach a separate report

Prospective Financial Statements

An accountant may be associated with prospective financial statements

- Prospective financial statements are the representation of a **responsible party**
- They provide an entity's financial position, results of operations, & changes in financial position for a future period of time

Prospective financial statements may be forecasts or projections

- **Forecasts** are based on what is expected to occur under normal circumstances
- **Projections** are based on what is expected to occur given one or more hypothetical assumptions

Forecasts may be prepared for general or limited use, but projections may only be prepared for limited use

- Statements prepared for **general use** will be used by those who are not necessarily directly negotiating with the responsible party
- Statements prepared for **limited use** will be used exclusively by those who are directly negotiating with the responsible party

Compilation Engagements

A compilation of prospective financial statements involves:

- Assembling the statements based on the responsible party's assumptions
- Reading the prospective financial statements & summaries of significant assumptions & accounting policies
- Considering whether statements & disclosures appear to conform to AICPA presentation guidelines

The accountant's compilation report will include

- Identification of the prospective statements presented by the responsible party
- Indication that the accountant has compiled the statements in accordance with AICPA standards
- A statement that a compilation is limited in scope & does not provide a basis for an opinion
- A statement that the prospective results may not be achieved
- A statement that the accountant is not responsible for updating the report
- Limitations on the use of the statements if the presentation is a projection

Examination Engagements

An examination of prospective financial statements involves

- Evaluating the preparation of the statements & the support underlying the assumptions
- Evaluating whether the presentation of the statements conforms to AICPA presentation guidelines

The accountant's standard report on an examination of prospective financial statements should include

- Identification of the prospective statements presented by the responsible party
- Indication that the examination was made in accordance with AICPA standards & a brief description of the nature of the examination
- The accountant's opinion as to presentation in conformity with AICPA guidelines & that the underlying assumptions provide a reasonable basis for the forecast or for the projection given the hypothetical assumptions
- A statement that the prospective results may not be achieved
- A statement that the accountant is not responsible for updating the report
- Limitations on the use of the statements if the presentation is a projection

Agreed-Upon Procedures

The accountant may apply agreed-upon procedures to prospective financial statements provided

- The accountant is independent
- The accountant & specified users agree upon the procedures
- The specified users take responsibility for the sufficiency of the procedures
- Use of the report is limited to the specified users

Reporting on Pro Forma Financial Information

Pro forma financial statements are based on historical information

- They consider an event or transaction that had not occurred as of the financial statement date
- They are restated to provide the information as if the event or transaction had occurred

The accountant will perform procedures to provide assurance that management's assumptions & presentation are reasonable

A report based on a review of pro forma financial information will identify the financial statements from which the historical information is derived

Review of Interim Financial Information

Accountant may perform a review of interim financial information

- Intent is to evaluate conformity with GAAP
- Review is basis for determining if material modification to the information is necessary

Procedures will include inquiries & APs

Presentation of information has impact on the accountant's report

- If the interim information is presented along with the financial statements, auditor adds a paragraph to audit report without modifying the opinion
- If the interim information is presented separately, auditor issues a separate review report

Governmental Auditing

Governmental audits refer to audits of

- Governmental entities
- Entities receiving governmental financial assistance

Audit is conducted under one or more of:

- Generally Accepted Auditing Standards (GAAS)
- Government Auditing Standards (GAS)
- The Single Audit Act (SAA)

GAS

Audits under GAS provide reasonable assurance of detecting material misstatements that

- Result from noncompliance with contract provisions or grant agreements
- Have a direct & material effect on the financial statements

GAS standards for fieldwork & reporting exceed standards under GAAS

The auditor's **written report** under GAS includes:

- An opinion on the financial statements
- Information regarding the consideration of internal control
- Information regarding the compliance with laws & regulations

GAS (continued)

As to the consideration of **internal control**, the report will indicate

- The scope of testing of controls
- An understanding of internal control
- An assessment of control risk
- Deficiencies in the design of internal controls

As to **compliance** with laws & regulations, the report will indicate

- Compliance is the responsibility of management
- Any material instances of fraud & illegal acts discovered

SAA

SAA applies to state & local governments, institutions of higher education, & other nonprofit organizations receiving federal financial assistance (ffa)

- Must engage auditor to perform single coordinated audit
- Audit relates to requirements of applicable ffa program

The report covers the financial statements, compliance with laws & regulations, & internal controls

In addition, the auditor reports on

- Compliance with general requirements applying to ffa programs
- Compliance with specific requirements of major federal programs
- Compliance with specific requirements of nonmajor federal programs tested

General requirements applying to ffa programs relate to national policy, including

- Providing a drug-free work place
- Prohibiting use of federal funds for partisan political activities
- Prohibiting violation of civil rights in a federally funded program
- Minimizing time between receipt & disbursement of federal funds

Major Federal Programs

Major federal programs are identified on the basis of:

- Expenditures exceeding certain amounts in relation to total expenditures of all ffa received during the year
- An analysis of risk assessment

Materiality is determined in relation to each program

Management identifies federal programs providing funding including:

- Funds received directly from federal agencies
- Funds received indirectly from federal agencies through state and local government agencies or nonprofit organizations

Auditor Responsibility

An auditor under the SAA must apply GAAS and GAS

When assessing risk, the auditor includes the risk of failure to modify the report despite noncompliance with the requirements of a specific program

- Inherent risk is modified to include the risk that material noncompliance could occur if there were no related controls
- Control risk is modified to include the risk that noncompliance may not be prevented or detected by the entity's controls
- Detection risk is modified to include the risk that audit procedures will not detect material noncompliance

The auditor reports on whether the entity has controls to provide reasonable assurance of compliance. The auditor:

- Evaluates the effectiveness of controls designed to detect noncompliance
- Determines if there are controls to ensure compliance in relation to billing of costs
- Documents procedures used to assess and test internal control

Testing for Compliance

When testing for compliance with requirements of major ffa programs, the auditor must consider:

- Activities that may or not be funded under a program
- Cost accounting principles that must be applied
- Procedures to minimize the time between receiving and spending of funds
- Compliance with the Davis-Bacon Act related to wages paid to laborers and mechanics
- Criteria related to eligibility for the programs
- Standards for the use and disposition of assets acquired with federal funds
- Requirements for contributions of resources by the recipient of federal funds
- Incurring of funded costs during the funding period
- Restrictions on contracting with parties disqualified from participation
- Recording and use of income generated from a federal program

Testing for Compliance (continued)

- Equitable treatment of displaced parties
- Reporting using standard forms
- Monitoring activities of subrecipients
- Special provisions of each federal program

Reports Under the SAA

Upon completion of an audit under the SAA, the auditor will issue a report that complies with requirements of GAAS and GAS as well as reports that are specific to the entity's federal awards.

Reporting requirements under the SAA include:

- Conformity with GAAP
- Fair presentation of the schedule of expenditures of federal awards
- Internal control as related to the financial statements and to major programs
- Compliance with laws, regulations, and provisions of contracts or grant agreements
- The schedule of federal awards listing total expenditures for each award
- Reportable conditions related to internal control over major programs
- Material noncompliance with laws, regulations, and contract or grant provisions
- Questioned costs in excess of $10,000
- Known fraud affecting a federal award

Summary of Relationship Among GAAS, GAS, & SAA

Procedures Required	*GAAS*	*GAS*	*SAA*
Audit of financial statements in accordance with specific standards	√	√	√
Compliance with laws & regulations	√	√	√
Internal controls	√	√	√
Compliance with general requirements			√
Compliance with specific requirements applicable to ffa programs			√
Understanding of specific internal controls relevant to ffa			√

Summary of Relationship Among GAAS, GAS, & SAA

Reports Issued	*GAAS*	*GAS*	*SAA*
Opinion on financial statements	√	√	√
Written report on compliance with laws & regulations		√	√
Written report on internal controls		√	√
Report on a list of total expenditures for each federal award			√
Prepare a schedule of reportable conditions, material noncompliance, questioned costs, and known fraud			√

Attestation Engagements

In attestation engagements, the accountant expresses a conclusion about the reliability of a written assertion of another party

Must comply with standards for attestation engagements

General Standards

1) Adequate technical training & proficiency in the attest function
2) Adequate knowledge of subject area covered by the assertion
3) Accept engagement only with reasonable likelihood that it can be completed successfully
    - The assertion must be capable of being evaluated against reasonable criteria
    - It must be capable of reasonable estimation or measurement against the criteria
4) Maintain independence in mental attitude
5) Exercise due professional care in performing engagement

Standards of Fieldwork

1) Adequate planning & supervision

2) Gather sufficient competent evidential matter as a reasonable basis for conclusions expressed

Standards of Reporting

1) Identify assertion reported on & character of engagement

2) State practitioners conclusion as to presentation of assertion in conformity with established or stated criteria